WATERCOLOUR
FOR ALL

18, 21, 37, 44, 76, 83
107, 109, 121

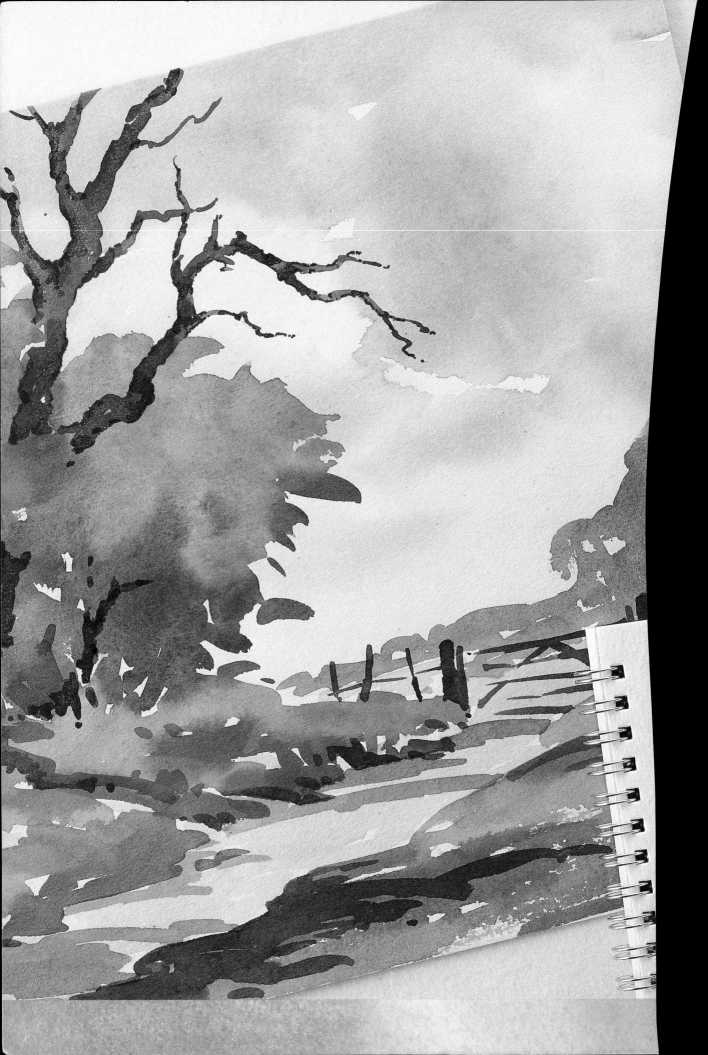

WATERCOLOUR FOR ALL

A Practical Guide for Beginners & Improvers

RAY CAMPBELL SMITH

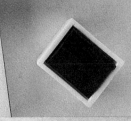

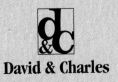

David & Charles

DEDICATION

To my family, my friends and fellow painters, and all those who share my love
of pure watercolour.

ACKNOWLEDGEMENTS

I would like to thank my editor, Alison Elks, for her help and advice, my son,
Paul, MA (Royal College of Art), BSc (London University) for his expert
photography of my paintings, Cherry Briers, editor of *Leisure Painter*, for
kindly allowing me to use material from that splendid magazine, Maureen
Gray, for her skilful typewriting and my wife, Eileen, for her constant
encouragement and support.

A DAVID & CHARLES BOOK

Copyright © Ray Campbell Smith 1993, 1998
First published 1993
First paperback edition 1998
Reprinted 1998

Ray Campbell Smith has asserted his right to be identified as author of this work in
accordance with the Copyright, Designs and Patents Act 1988.

A catalogue record for this book is available from the British Library.

ISBN (hardback) 0 7153 0055 5
ISBN (paperback) 0 7153 0713 4

Typeset by Ace Filmsetting, Frome, Somerset
and printed in Hong Kong by Wing King Tong Co Ltd
for David & Charles
Brunel House   Newton Abbot   Devon

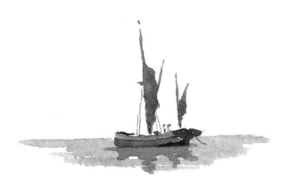

Contents

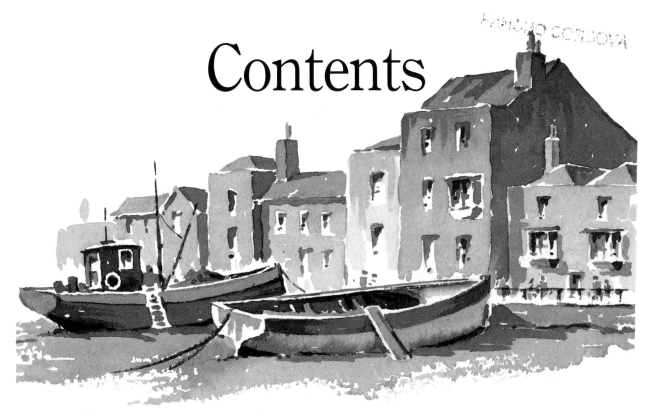

INTRODUCTION   6
● Demonstration: Christmas Eve   12

1 MATERIALS AND THEIR USES   14
   ● Demonstration: Bluestone Farm   22

2 COLOUR — THEORY AND PRACTICE   24
   ● Demonstration: Dunsfold Church   34

3 PUTTING IT IN PERSPECTIVE   36
   ● Demonstration: Calm Anchorage   46

4 COMPOSITION AND BALANCE   50
   ● Demonstration: Cottages at Filkins   60

5 CHOOSING AND DEVELOPING SUBJECTS   64
   ● Demonstration: Kentish Farmyard   70

6 ALL ABOUT WASHES   72
   ● Demonstration: The Grand Canal   80

7 MORE WATERCOLOUR TECHNIQUES   82
   ● Demonstration: Farm Buildings   90

8 MIST AND MYSTERY   92
   ● Demonstration: Trees in the Mist   100

9 PAINTING IN THE OPEN   102
   ● Demonstration: Mr Perkins Gardening 114

10 TO SUM UP   116
   ● Demonstration: Fog and Drizzle   124

GLOSSARY   126
INDEX   127

Introduction

M ost small children love drawing and painting and their untutored images often have an appeal and a simple charm of their own. This inborn creative urge is too often extinguished by unimaginative and unsympathetic teaching at school. Happily, more and more people are forgetting their early disappointments and are turning to art as a richly rewarding pastime and a means of self expression. The question soon arises as to which medium to adopt. Unfortunately many are put off even trying their hand at watercolour because of its reputation for difficulty and unpredictability and even those braver spirits, who have really given it a go, are sometimes frustrated and disappointed with their results. This is a pity because watercolour is a wonderful medium, ideally suited to the fresh and atmospheric interpretation of landscape subjects and, what is more, most aspiring artists can master its complexities if offered the right sort of help.

BEGINNINGS

What, then, is the way ahead? Can we pinpoint the basic difficulties of the medium and learn to overcome them? I believe we can. Of course, all sorts of factors go into the making of a successful painting and we shall be considering these in turn throughout this book. The first and perhaps the most important skill to learn in order to produce successful watercolour paintings is the correct application of the paint.

Watercolour is a transparent medium and its real beauty lies in the clarity and freshness of the applied paint, so that the white of the paper shines through. These marvellous qualities are very easily lost, and that is why one sees so many watercolour paintings in which the colours are drab and muddy and totally lacking in sparkle. However brilliant the composition, however well observed the tone values, if freshness and clarity have been lost, failure is the inevitable result. What must we do to make absolutely sure they are preserved?

It is surprising how many watercolourists dip their brush in the water jar, then into the pan of colour and apply the paint directly to the paper. If more water or pigment is required, the brush returns to the jar or pan to be replenished. This is not the way to achieve freshness and clarity. Far better results are obtained if a wash is first prepared. Pour a little water into one of the wells in the paintbox lid or mixing palette, add paint and mix as required until the

desired colour and tone (*see* Glossary) are obtained. Only then should the mixture be applied to the paper. If this simple operation is carried out properly, the resulting wash will, on drying, be fresh and clear.

The wash should be applied to the paper as quickly as possible and then left strictly alone. So often painters go on pushing the wash about, sometimes to make it fit exactly into some complex shape, all the time sacrificing freshness. Sometimes they find the tone is not deep enough and add more pigment; sometimes it is too deep and pigment has to be removed, with the result that still more freshness and clarity are lost. Until you are experienced enough to judge the tone of your washes with confidence, it is well worth while testing them out on an offcut of similar paper, always bearing in mind that watercolour fades appreciably on drying and that washes should therefore appear too deep-toned when first applied.

It is often believed that areas of deep tone are bound to lose clarity because of the concentration of pigment they demand, but this need not be so. Loss of clarity will only occur if the colour is put on with too dry a brush, but if the paint is applied boldly in the form of a rich wash, all should be well. Of course, if too many colours are mixed together in a single wash, muddiness will result, but this is another matter and one we shall be examining in a later chapter (*see* page 72).

Some of the most admired watercolour paintings are executed very loosely, with

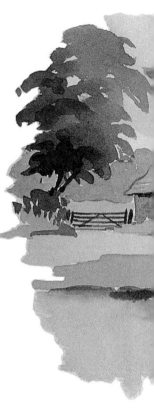

SUMMERFORD FARM, WITHYHAM
I painted this impression of a typical Kentish farm in about twenty minutes to demonstrate to a group of students how a fairly complex subject might be captured quickly and directly without too much labouring after detail. It is an excellent discipline to set yourself a time limit, particularly if you feel your work is too tight and meticulous – the speed with which you have to work makes you concentrate on essentials and leaves no time for fiddling!

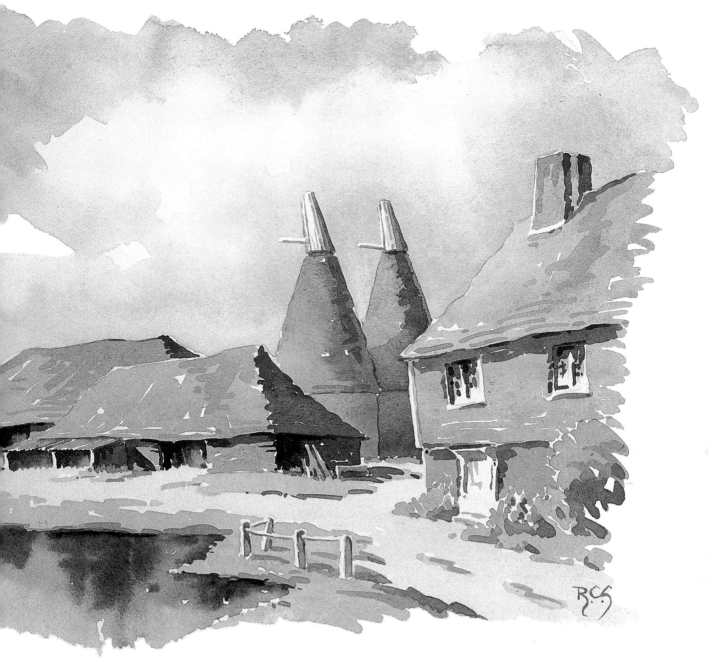

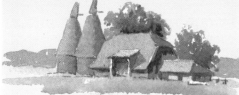
little attempt at portraying detail. This is not only because the artists have been more concerned with feeling and atmosphere than they have with mere accuracy, but also because they know that their quickly and boldly applied washes will preserve the freshness and clarity of their work.

One of the reasons that some painters produce tired and overworked results is that they tend to experiment on their paper. They are not sure, until the paint is applied, whether it is producing the effect they want or not. This approach nearly always leads to modification and consequent lack of freshness.

The most important stage of all in successful watercolour painting is the mental translation of the observed image into watercolour terms and this is where skill and

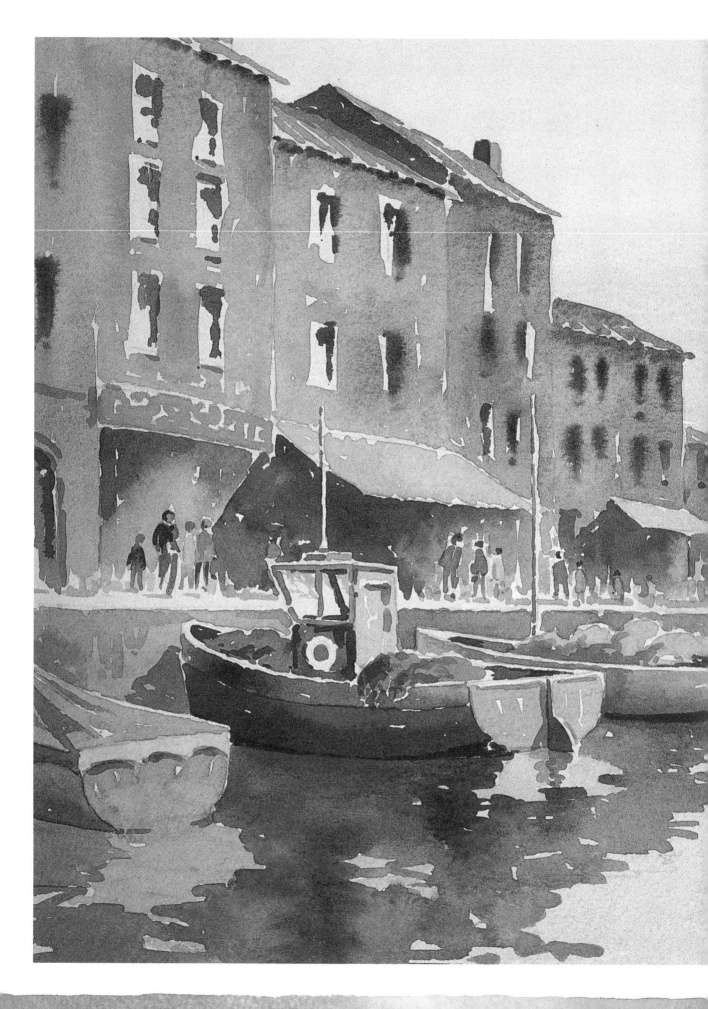

WATERCOLOUR FOR ALL

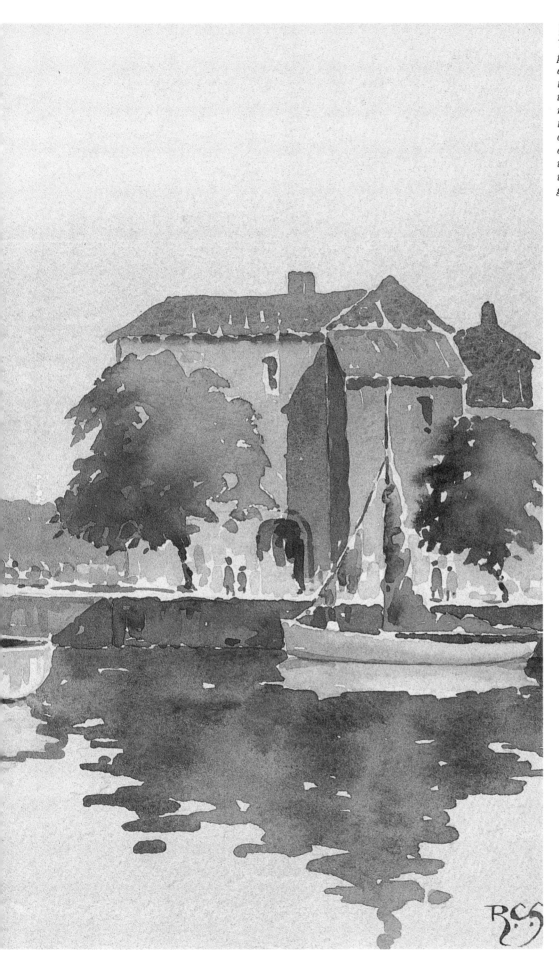

This attractive French port is always full of life and colour. Although there is plenty of colour in this painting, I resisted the temptation to cram in too many competing hues. The overall feeling is one of warmth which contrasts with the glimpse of blue-grey distance.

INTRODUCTION

9

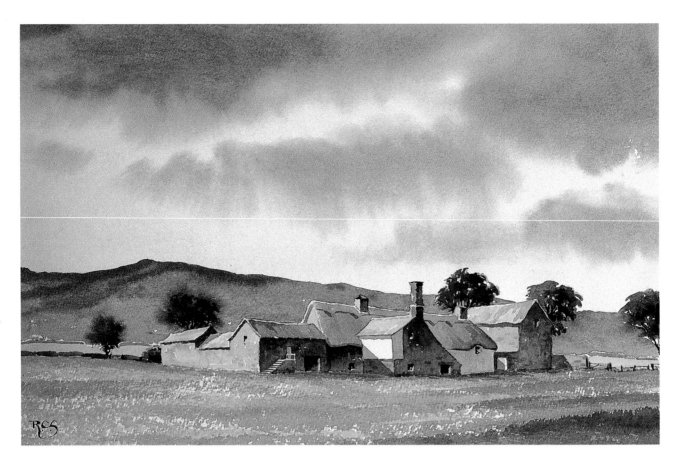

experience come into play. Beginners, ever optimistic, frequently entertain the hope that some magic in the medium itself will enable them to obtain the effect they so desire. Despite the happy accidents of art folklore, this rarely happens. The proper approach is to analyse the problems posed and think out ways of overcoming them.

To illustrate the point I am trying to make, let us take the case of an inexperienced artist tackling a field of grass in the foreground of his painting. He will probably spend a little time mixing the right colour green and will apply it over the whole area of the field. Even if he has succeeded in getting the tone and colour right, he will realise at once that the result is altogether too flat and featureless. He will then start putting in little tufts of grass, to break up the excessive smoothness, and will soon find he is trying to paint individual blades of grass. The areas between his tufts, by contrast, will start to look even more featureless than before and he will feel constrained to apply the same detailed treatment to them. Before he understands what is happening, the whole foreground will become tired and overworked and, in all probability, thoroughly dull and muddy.

There are several ways to remedy this, depending on his style and approach, but all of them require forethought and planning.

DARTMOOR FARM

My object in this painting was to capture something of the brooding atmosphere of Dartmoor under lowering storm clouds. At the same time I wanted to do justice to the splendid old farmhouse which I sketched with some accuracy.

I applied a wash of palest raw sienna to the whole of the sky and then dropped in a mixture of burnt sienna and ultramarine for the brownish-grey clouds. The slope of my board caused some downward flow, suggesting an approaching rain squall. I then added some deeper shadow, wet in wet (see glossary), for the heavier clouds.

The shoulder of moorland was a deep wash of ultramarine and light red, with a little raw sienna added to the lower slopes and some darker shadow at the top.

The foreground was a broken wash of raw sienna and a little Payne's grey, applied with quick, horizontal strokes of a large brush. When this was dry, I added some texture with a rather drier brush, to suggest the rough nature of the surface.

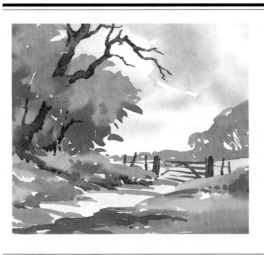

Whatever he does, he should not begin to paint his foreground until he has first decided upon his plan of campaign and his strategy. If, for example, he favours a loose approach, he may decide that a broken wash, applied with bold, horizontal strokes, will give him the effect he wants. The strings of little white dots of untouched paper which such a wash produces, particularly on rough paper, may suggest masses of seed heads in the grass or simply indicate texture. With growing experience, he will be able to modify the colour and the tone of his wash, to represent variations in the appearance of the grass, without losing either freshness or clarity. A second texturing wash might also be applied and, although in general terms it is usually better to say what you have to say in one wash rather than two, not much freshness will be lost provided the texturing wash is applied equally boldly and quickly, so that the original wash is not disturbed.

In the early stages of a painting the bold approach may not produce precisely the effects you are aiming at, but even if the result is not quite what you had in mind, it is likely to be more effective as a watercolour painting than the overworked alternative. With growing experience you will gradually get closer to nature, particularly if you remember that it is not a photographic image of the subject that you are after, but a fresh interpretation of it in watercolour terms.

WINTER ON THE YORKSHIRE MOORS
The bold and loose application of liquid paint can help you capture dramatic sky effects, as this quick impression of lowering clouds shows. I applied a dilute wash of Payne's grey over the whole of the sky area, down to the line of snow-clad hills. Into this a pale wash of ultramarine and light red was dropped to indicate the softer clouds, and this was followed by a much stronger mix for the heavy clouds at top left.

The isolated farm buildings were placed on the right of the painting to provide tonal balance. The foreground snow, in cloud shadow, was a loosely applied wash of Payne's grey.

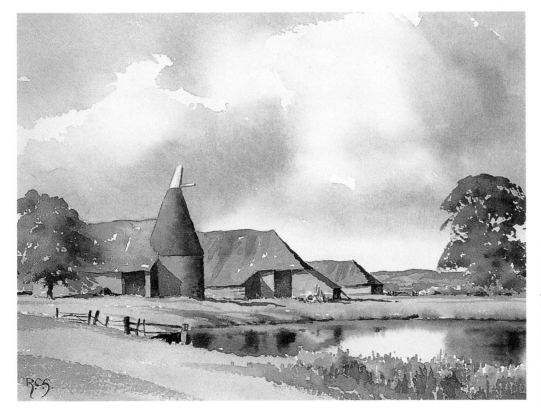

FARM NEAR SHIPBOURNE
This rural subject has been treated fairly directly, with most of the passages comprising simple washes of transparent colour. Much of the foreground is a flat wash of raw sienna to which broken washes have been added to suggest shadow and texture.

CHRISTMAS EVE

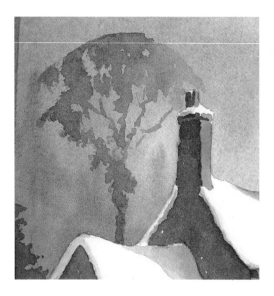

In this Christmas card scene, the crispness of the snow-covered farmhouse, the five-bar gate and the other foreground features contrast with the misty distance in which the dim, vertical forms of conifers can just be made out. The house is viewed at an oblique angle, enabling two elevations to be seen, and their difference in tone helps to give the building a three-dimensional look. The lines of the house, the hedge and the lane all lead the eye towards the patch of radiance in the sky, beneath which I later decided to place a small, dark figure, to create a focal point.

Palette

raw sienna
light red
ultramarine
Payne's grey
burnt sienna

STAGE 1

I began by sketching in the principal lines of the house, the gate and the lane. The next step was to establish the warm tones of the evening sky and indicate the misty trees, while the background wash was still sufficiently wet. This technique is known as 'wet in wet'. For an operation of this sort it is, of course, necessary to prepare the washes in advance – there is no time to start mixing up paint once the basic wash has been applied. The area of pale sky was dilute raw sienna warmed with light red, and the deeper tones were a warm grey, achieved by mixing ultramarine and light red. I applied these washes quickly, allowing them to merge softly. I then began to put in the more distant tree forms, wet in wet, using a slightly stronger mix of the same grey. I added a little Payne's grey on the

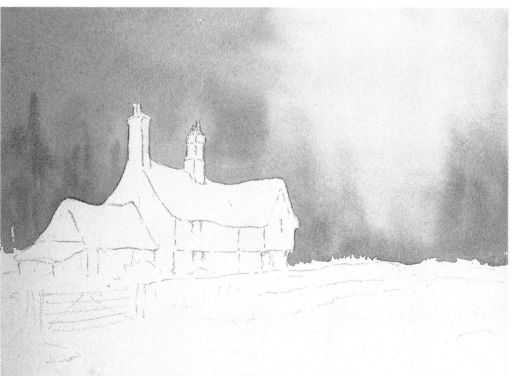

left and indicated the conifers here with a little more definition. At this stage I decided to add the foreground bush on the right, to help balance the main tonal weight, which lay on the left. This addition also helped to prevent the eye following the line of the road right off the paper.

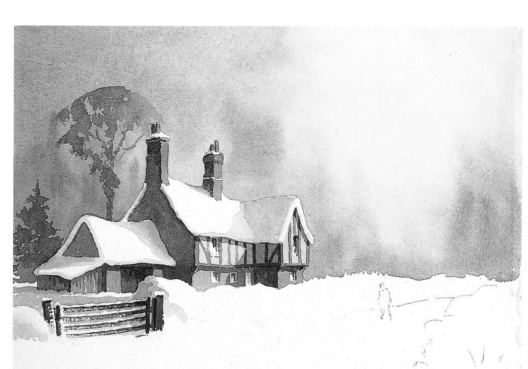

The creamy colour of the Arches watercolour paper was ideal for the snow – anything too dead white would have required warming, to accord with the light in the sky. The snow shadows also needed some warmth and I used a pale wash of ultramarine and light red. In wintry scenes such as this everything has to be painted in deeper tones than usual in order to make the snow shine by contrast. The brickwork was painted in varying combinations of burnt sienna and light red. A much deeper mixture of the same colours, plus ultramarine, served for the shadowed elevations. Notice the warm reflected light on the left-facing gables.

When I had finished painting the house, its crisp treatment rather divorced it from its misty background and it seemed to me that some intermediate forms were needed to link the two together. I accordingly painted in the muted shapes of the conifer and the deciduous tree on the left.

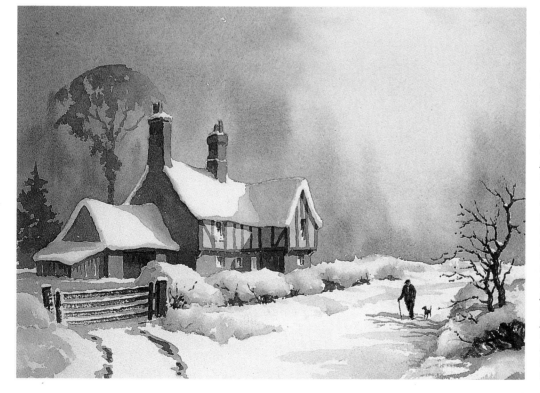

STAGE 3

I prepared another wash of ultramarine and light red and applied it quickly and boldly to indicate the shadows in the snow, softening the edges here and there with clear water. This gave direction to the road and helped to describe the form of the lumpy snow resting on the hedge.

A wash of raw sienna and ultramarine was used for the glimpse of hedge under its weight of snow and a darker mix of the same two colours served for the odd twig, the wheel tracks by the gate and the bare bush on the right. Finally, I put in the figures of the old man and his dog in still deeper tones to make them stand out against their pale background.

1 Materials and their Uses

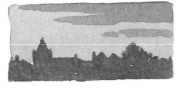

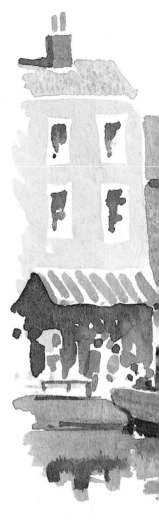

The first step in mastering watercolour technique is, of course, the purchase of the proper equipment and it is vital to ensure that this is not a false step. Failure to seek informed advice, or the acceptance of advice that is not entirely disinterested, can easily result in the acquisition of unsuitable materials, unnecessary expense or, in all probability, both.

The proprietors of most art shops offer sound and helpful advice, but it has to be remembered that they have a vested interest in selling the more expensive items and these are not always the most suitable. I have come across numerous instances in which inexperienced painters have been persuaded to buy magnificent presentation watercolour sets containing dozens of pans of paint. These sets are not only extremely expensive but in my view are positively harmful. The bewildering array of pigments leads to confusion and to paintings in which there are so many unrelated colours that all feeling of unity and cohesion is lost. I was once given an enormous watercolour set in a handsome hardwood case containing forty-eight pans of colour; I still have it in its original pristine condition. What I use instead is a simple black enamelled box containing just a few pans of colour, finding this ample for my needs and far more manageable and portable.

We must, however, distinguish between expensive necessities – paints, brushes and paper – and expensive frills. It really pays to buy the best 'necessities' we can afford, for watercolour painting is quite difficult enough without adding to our problems by using second-rate materials.

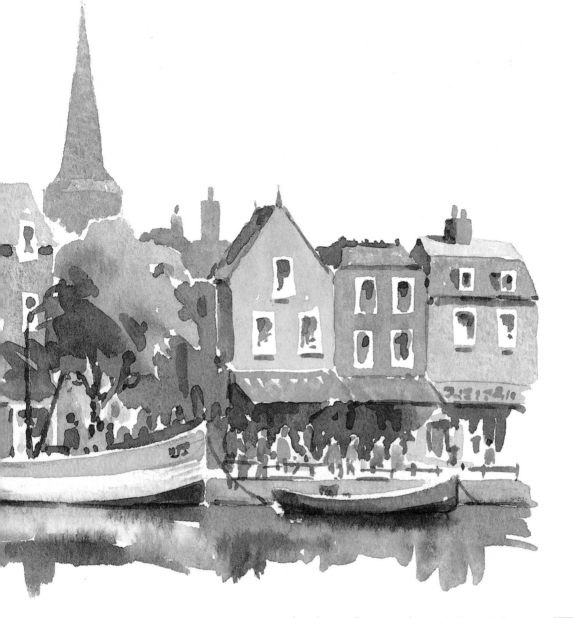

PALETTE RANGE

There is a definite advantage in using a small number of colours in your work. Not only do you get to know the handling properties of a narrow range much more quickly – and colours *do* vary in this respect – but where combinations of just a few colours occur in all parts of the painting, that painting 'hangs together' far more satisfactorily. The question then arises as to which colours to buy. This is very difficult to answer for so much depends on individual preference and taste. We all see colour differently, though in most cases only marginally so, and experienced artists tend to stick to a specific range that suits their particular needs. Naturally, much will depend upon the type of subject matter you favour. Flower painters, for example, will need a selection of brilliant colours if they are to capture the more spectacular hues of nature. Landscape painters, on the other hand, are often more interested in subtlety and frequently obtain telling effects by understatement.

My own palette for landscape work is shown right. To my basic five I often add Payne's grey, burnt umber and alizarin crimson for particular types of subject. For the brighter colours of the Mediterranean scene I add cadmium yellow and cadmium orange as well.

I remain a firm advocate of the limited palette, and frequently use just three colours in my work – light red, raw sienna and ultramarine. After all, these are simply variations of the three primaries, red, yellow and blue, and can produce an impressive array of secondary and tertiary colours. Quite simply, secondary colours contain just two primaries (green, for example, is a mixture of yellow and blue) while the tertiaries contain all three primary colours. Some of these combinations produce colours of exceptional beauty and subtlety.

My Basic Palette

Light red
Raw sienna
Burnt sienna
Ultramarine
Prussian blue

Extras:
Payne's grey
Burnt umber
Alizarin crimson
Cadmium yellow
Cadmium orange

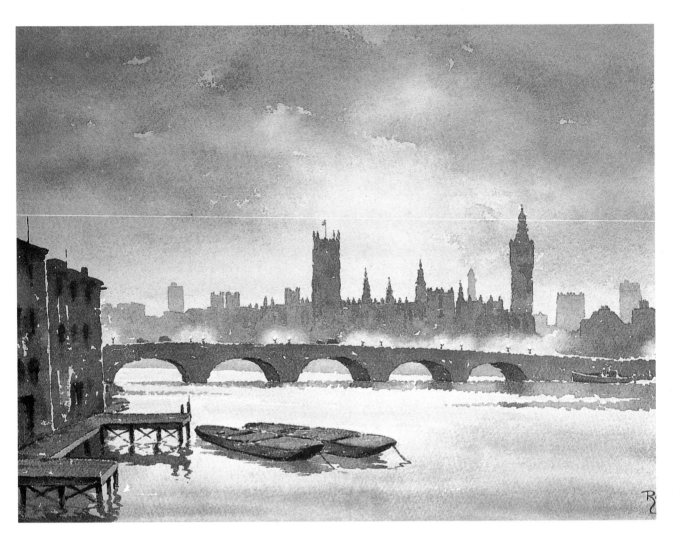

CHOOSING PAINTS

Colours vary in their durability and are coded by the manufacturers according to their colour-fastness. Fortunately the fugitive or unreliable colours of Victorian times have been superseded by more reliable pigments. Colours come in two qualities, artists' and students', the former naturally being the more expensive. Artists' colours contain more finely ground and in some cases more costly pigments and are superior in strength and clarity. The choice between the two grades is a matter for the individual, but my feeling is that one needs all the help available in the difficult yet fascinating business of watercolour painting and so I opt for the artist's quality. They *are* more expensive, but it has to be borne in mind that the watercolour medium is far more economical of pigment than oil or acrylic and the difference in cost per painting cannot be very significant.

The next choice is between pan and tube colour, and this again is a matter of personal preference. If you prefer pans, make sure they are kept reasonably moist by the periodic addition of clear water, for nothing is more frustrating – or harder on brushes – than trying to coax reluctant pigment from dried up pans. Many of those who prefer tubes squeeze out small blobs of colour round the edge of their mixing palettes, and wash the whole lot off at the end of each painting session – a very wasteful procedure. My own practice is to squeeze the tube paint into the appropriate pan before painting begins. In this way one always has moist paint to use, the new paint freshens up the old and nothing is lost.

BRUSHES

Good and lively brushwork is an essential ingredient in successful watercolour painting, yet it is a skill that too many painters fail to develop. This failure often stems from too much detailed drawing, for then the painting simply becomes a mechanical process of filling in the areas between carefully drawn outlines, leaving no scope for the expressive use of the brush.

Good brushwork naturally demands good brushes and the best obtainable are made of Kolinsky sable. Unfortunately these have become extremely expensive and

WESTMINSTER BRIDGE
Just three colours were used in this impression of an evening sky over Westminster – raw sienna, light red and ultramarine. These three colours appear, in varying proportions, in all parts of the scene and consequently the painting has a unity which the introduction of alien hues could easily have destroyed. Such a limited palette is not, of course, always possible or desirable, but when a warm sky, such as this, strongly influences the scene below, then the colours used for the sky are often all that is needed.

beyond the reach of most painters. On the credit side, alternatives have been developed and some of these are extremely good. My favourites are manufactured from a mixture of sable and man-made fibre, and while it has to be said that no compromise can quite match the real thing, they are excellent in their way and enable one to produce bold and lively brushwork.

The next question that has to be decided is that of size. Inexperienced painters always go for the smaller sizes, partly because they are less expensive and partly because they are believed to be more manageable. Sadly,

the influence of these smaller brushes is all on the wrong side, for they tend to encourage preoccupation with detail and are virtually useless for producing the full washes upon which success in watercolour so much depends. True, in the early stages the use of larger brushes may well cause handling difficulties, but with time and practice they will wean you away from obsessive detail and towards bigger and bolder effects. In short, they will help you to 'loosen up' and you will come to realise that feeling and verve in painting are of far more value than precision and accuracy.

MY WATERCOLOUR BRUSHES

It is not possible to lay down recommended sizes for brushes, for so much depends upon the individual's style and scale of painting, but you may find it helpful to know what I normally use. Most of my work varies in size from quarter imperial (11 × 15in/28 × 38 cm), to half imperial (15 × 22in/38 × 56cm); for this I use the brushes below.

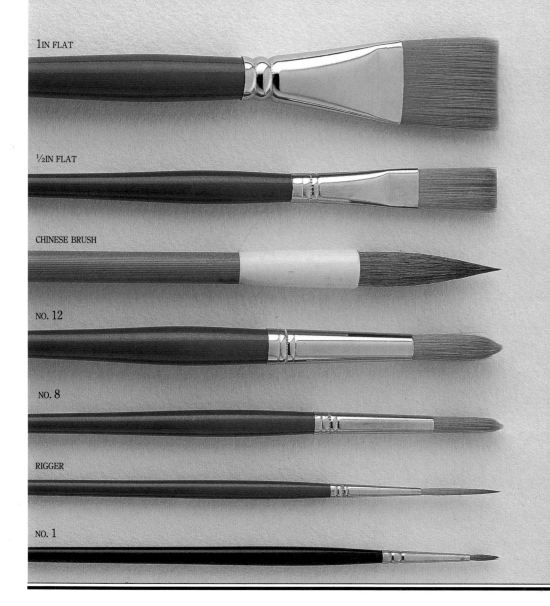

1IN FLAT

½IN FLAT

CHINESE BRUSH

NO. 12

NO. 8

RIGGER

NO. 1

TWO 1IN (2.5CM) AND TWO ½IN (1.25CM) FLATS
I use these for skies and other large passages. They are chisel-ended when bought, and I must confess I modify them by carefully rounding the sharp angled edges with nail scissors. This enables me to achieve a pleasantly broken edge to each brushstroke.

CHINESE BRUSH
Mine is large and round, of some antiquity. I use it for quick and bold modification of sky washes whilst they are still wet.

NO. 12 AND NO. 8
I use these brushes for objects within the landscape – trees, buildings, boats and so on. I make a conscious effort to use the larger brush wherever possible, as this prevents me becoming involved in fiddly detail.

RIGGER
I use this mainly for its original purpose – to paint the rigging on boats.

NO. 1
This is used for adding my initials!

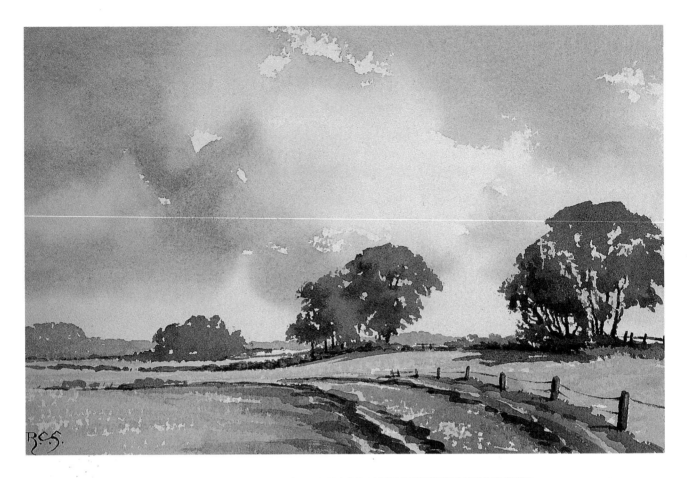

BEACHED BOAT

This quick sketch was made with an aquarelle pencil. The graphite is soluble in water so the marks it makes may be softened with a wet brush.

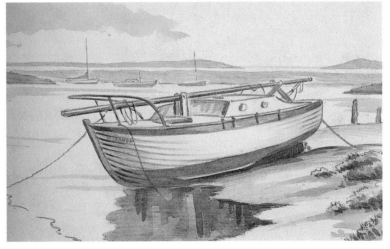

FARM TRACK

The most important part of a watercolour landscape is a fresh and lively sky. Fortunately it is the feature we normally tackle first and if it is a disaster, we can make a fresh start without too much loss of time. Most failures are due to timidity or attempted alteration or both, so it pays to cultivate a bold approach and resist the temptation to 'tidy up'. In this quick study, three washes – for sunlit cloud, cloud shadow and blue sky – were applied in quick succession and then left. I made no attempt to fill in the little areas of white which often result from working at speed.

RHODODENDRON

Watercolour is the ideal medium for capturing the fragile forms of flowers. I used a NOT paper for this quick study of a species rhododendron blossom, using pale combinations of alizarin crimson, light red and ultramarine for its subdued yet subtle pinks and Payne's grey with a little raw sienna for the dark leaves.

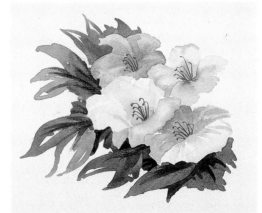

PAPER

There are many watercolour papers on the market. The best of these are made from pure cotton rag and are rather expensive, but cheaper papers made of wood pulp are available, and the best of these are admirable, representing excellent value. Papers are classified according to their surface texture and their weight. Although most papers produced today are machine made, I prefer those that have the look of a hand-made finish – a random grain which I find infinitely preferable to a mechanical, repetitive type of finish.

Papers vary considerably in the hardness of their surface. The softer papers, containing less size in their dressing, are more absorbent and washes quickly sink in, making it difficult to make alterations. The harder papers are slower to dry and although in watercolour alteration should be avoided if possible, they permit careful changes to be made, except, perhaps in passages (ie areas) of pale, clear washes, such as the sky or expanses of water.

Full, liquid washes make the lighter weight papers cockle badly in use and this gives rise to uneven drying, with its attendant problems of patchiness and flowering. These papers have to be stretched before use. The heavier papers resist serious cockling but they are, of course, more expensive. Weight is expressed in pounds (or grammes) to the ream of Imperial size and the principal weights are 90lb (190gm), 140lb (295gm), 200lb (421gm), 240lb (504gm) and 300lb (632gm).

It makes good sense to experiment with the available papers until you find one that really suits your style and then stick to it. Papers vary considerably in the way they accept paint and you will produce better work if you are using a paper with which you are familiar.

You should always take great care of your watercolour paper and ensure its surface is protected against damage. Although good quality paper appears robust, its surface can easily be abraded or scratched. Such damage only becomes obvious when a wash is applied and unwelcome dark marks appear.

PAPER TEXTURE

Papers are classified according to their surface texture and their weight. There are three types of surface:

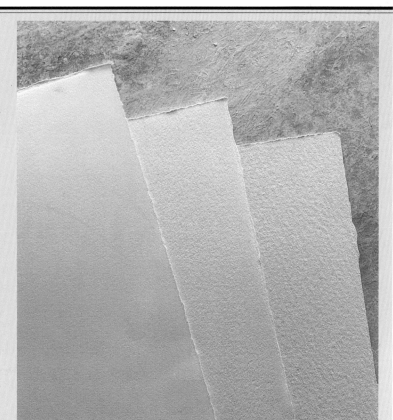

SMOOTH

Also known as HP, which stands for hot press. The effect of applying a heated press to the paper in the manufacturing process is to give it an extremely smooth finish with no visible surface indentations.

USES: the very smooth surface of this paper makes it ideal for pen and ink work, as its lack of texture enables the nib to glide smoothly over the surface without snagging. It is less suitable for watercolour because its lack of 'tooth' can easily cause the brush to slide over the surface without making an effective statement.

NOT

Also known as CP, which stands for cold press. This means that the paper has been finished by the application of an unheated press which reduces the surface irregularities but leaves some patina.

USES: this is the paper surface most commonly used by watercolourists, because it provides them with sufficient surface texture without the problems they may experience with the greater irregularities of the 'rough' grade.

ROUGH

This is a more textured paper, originally prepared by omitting the pressing stage altogether. Today, most rough papers are given their surface grain by the application of textured presses.

USES: this paper is ideal for dry brushwork and the application of broken washes, as its rough surface facilitates the use of such methods. These techniques are dealt with in more detail in Chapter 7.

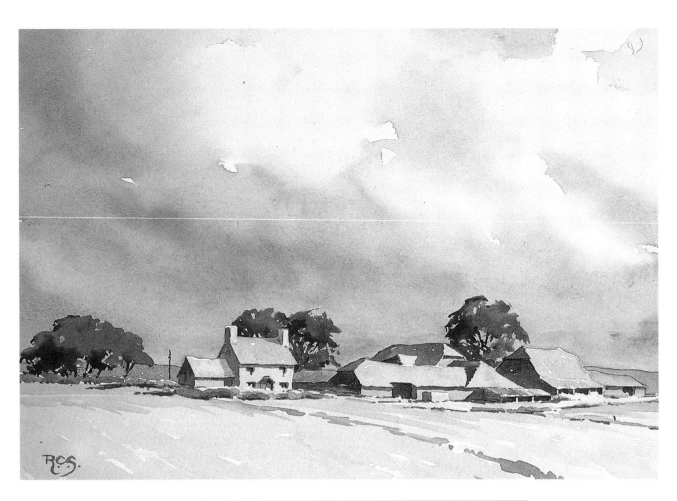

STRETCHING PAPER

Paper weighing less than 200lb should be 'stretched' before use. This prevents the paper cockling when wet washes are applied. Here are four easy stages to be followed when stretching paper:

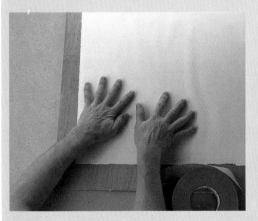

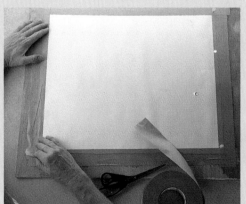

1 Completely immerse the sheet of paper, keeping it as flat as possible, in cold water. Leave it to soak for five minutes.

2 Remove the paper, allowing excess water to drip off,

then lay it flat on a drawing board an inch or two (2–5cm) larger.

3 Carefully smooth away air bubbles with your hand or a soft cloth until the paper lies flat.

4 Secure the complete length of all four edges with brown gummed paper tape. For extra security some artists also fasten the corners using drawing pins.

Once the paper is dry, it is ready to use. The painting is done with the paper still attached to the board it has been stretched on. Carefully cut off with a knife when completely dry.

WILTSHIRE FARM

This is an example of lively brushwork on a smooth, or hot press, paper. With a rough paper, the unevenness of the surface assists a brush held at an oblique angle to achieve a broken mark which can represent, for example, the ragged outline of foliage. A smoother paper demands a different technique in which the quality of the brushwork is all-important.

In this study, a strong sun was illuminating the farm buildings, which stood out against a backdrop of heavy grey cloud to produce a dramatic tonal contrast. This was the effect I tried to capture.

EXERCISES TO TRY

Here are a few simple watercolour sketches which you may care to try out for yourself. They contain some of the basic brushstrokes and should be copied boldly and freely. I hope you will find them more fun to do than some of the exercises commonly set.

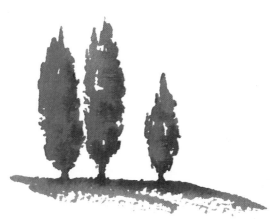

Three full, vertical brushstrokes on rough paper produced these quick impressions of cypress trees and two horizontal strokes the ground beneath them. The addition of a little deeper tone into the wet paint indicated shadow.

The quick application of a liquid wash on rough paper produces a broken wash, useful in suggesting texture.

A continuous wash of blue/grey, with some brush drawing, decreases in tone to the right, to suggest distant trees and hedges. This technique was used for

the distance in Snow over the Downs *(see page 27). The progressive addition of water to the wash will, of course, lighten the tone.*

Here a broken wash of pale raw sienna suggests the texture of the foreground field of cereal. A deeper wash of grey-green was applied

loosely on the rough paper, the texture of which helped to produce the broken edge.

BLUESTONE FARM, NORFOLK

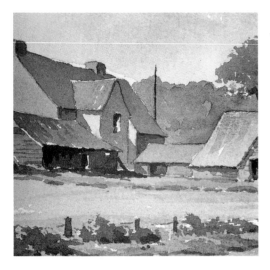

O ne of the things that always strikes me about the Norfolk scene is the immensity of its skies above the broad sweep of the East Anglian terrain, and I have tried to capture something of that feeling in this painting. Here the sky consists mainly of a lively formation of cumulus cloud – that most paintable of all cloud types – and to add emphasis to it I have adopted a low horizon. Not *too* low, for there is plenty of interest in the group of typically Norfolk farm buildings below their stand of sheltering trees.

Palette
raw sienna
light red
ultramarine
Payne's grey
burnt sienna

STAGE 1

My first step is always to make several rough sketches of my subject and then enlarge the most promising to the size of the planned painting. This is the one I like best and although the buildings are rather strung out in a straight line, there is sufficient overlapping for them to relate to one another, and the farmhouse, set at an attractive angle, is facing conveniently into the painting.

I always begin by painting the sky, partly because it is usually the lightest part of the scene and partly because it strongly influences every other part of the painting. With a sky such as this I favour a bold treatment, with some washes merging together and others remaining hard edged, to provide interest and contrast.

Here I began by preparing three generous washes, one for the sunlit areas of cloud, one for the cloud

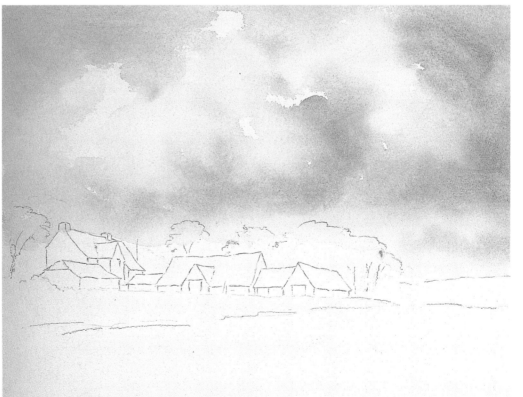

shadows and one for the blue of the sky. The washes were (1) dilute raw sienna, (2) ultramarine and light red, and (3) ultramarine with just a touch of light red respectively. I applied them, in that order, in quick succession. Putting the heaviest cloud shadow on the right helped to balance the main weight of the composition, which is on the left. The pale sky just above the horizon was a slightly richer raw sienna wash. Immediately the washes were in place, I modified them a little with another large brush, but resisted the temptation to over-elaborate and tidy up – a bold, fresh effect is always better than a neat and timid one!

STAGE 2

With the light coming from the left and falling on the roofs of the farm buildings, I wanted to ensure that the trees behind afforded plenty of tonal contrast. I therefore prepared fairly strong washes of Payne's grey with varying amounts of raw and burnt sienna, and applied them with the side of the brush to obtain the broken outline of the foliage. While these were still moist I added stronger versions of the same mixes to indicate the shaded areas.

The far distance was a flat wash of ultramarine tinged with light red. The middle distance bank of trees was a rather stronger mixture of the same colours with just a hint of raw sienna added, applied wet in wet, and a little shadow applied on the right.

The basic washes for the foreground fields were palest burnt sienna and light red for the plough-land and a broken wash of Payne's grey and raw sienna for the rough grass.

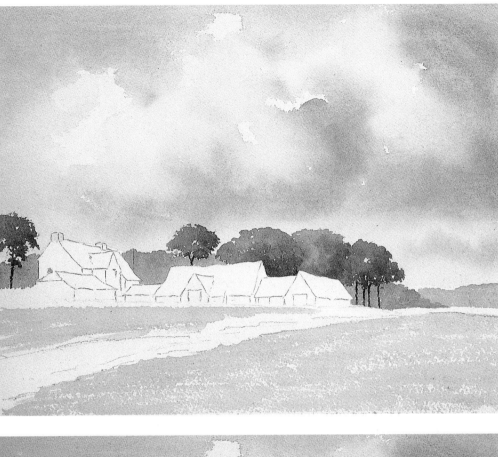

STAGE 3

I now began to paint the warm colours of the Norfolk pantiles, using raw sienna and light red with just a touch of green (made up of Payne's grey and raw sienna) to suggest the moss and algae that usually cling to the lower courses. When this was dry, I added a little texture in slightly deeper tones with brush strokes which followed the slope of the roofs. I then deepened the shaded areas of some of the trees to make the buildings register more effectively. As always, I paid close attention to the shadows of the buildings which I painted in deep tones.

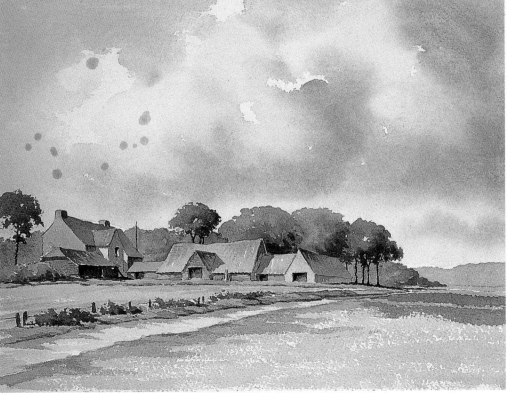

I added some cloud shadow to the field on the right and a little texturing in the form of a pale broken wash to the plough-land on the left. The line of rough hedge and fence posts, put in with a smaller brush, and a shadow on the track completed the painting.

2 Colour – Theory and Practice

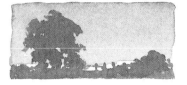

Colour is of vital interest to the watercolourist, for well-chosen colours can make all the difference between the success or failure of a painting. People vary in their feeling for colour and in their appreciation of its subtleties; some have a natural response to it and an instinctive understanding of its complexities, while others have to rely on a more analytical and methodical approach.

PRIMARY, SECONDARY AND TERTIARY COLOURS

We have already mentioned primary, secondary and tertiary colours and we now need to go just a little further into colour theory. We know that the three primary colours are red, yellow and blue and we know that any combination of two of these primaries will produce what are called secondary colours. Thus red and yellow make orange, yellow and blue make green, blue and red make violet – the orange, green and violet being the secondary colours. These vary according to the proportions of the primaries used and if there is, for example, more red than yellow in the first combination, a warmer orange will result.

Tertiary colours result from mixing the secondaries or from mixing all three primaries and are sometimes termed 'broken colours'. If the three primary constituents are mixed in more or less equal proportions, dull greys and browns tend to emerge, but if one primary or secondary colour is allowed to predominate, rich, subtle and often beautiful colours may result, and it is these that are of the greatest value in landscape painting.

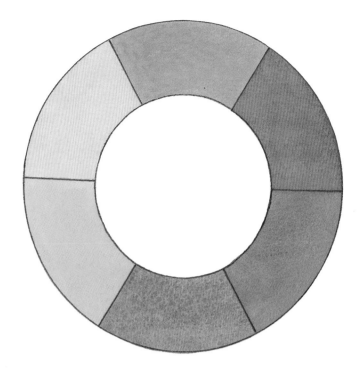

Here is an example of the simplest form of colour wheel, in which the three primaries – red, yellow and blue – are separated by the three secondaries – orange, green and violet. Each secondary is obtained by mixing the two adjacent primaries. Thus orange is obtained by mixing red and yellow, green by mixing yellow and blue, and violet by mixing blue and red.

The two primaries, red and yellow, combine to produce orange, a secondary colour. When a small quantity of blue is mixed with the orange, a warm and subtle brown results. This is a tertiary or broken colour and would be useful in landscape work, for old brick, autumn foliage, plough-land and so on.

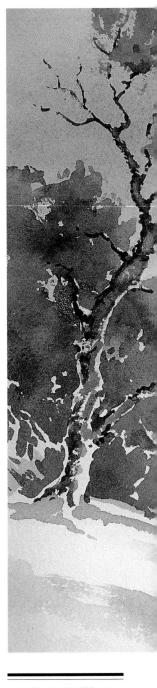

Blues and greys tend to recede and warm colours advance. But beware! Dark colours of whatever temperature are inclined to jump forward, especially if the foreground is much paler.

Here the pale blue-grey hills really do recede, helped by the much deeper tones of the foreground.

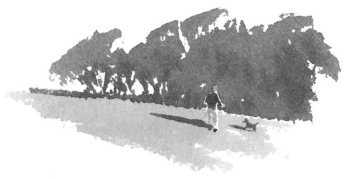

An example of the way in which a colour registers strongly against its complementary. The small, red figure stands out boldly against its green landscape setting.

COLOUR TEMPERATURE

Colour temperature is an aspect to be considered if we wish to achieve a feeling of depth in our work. Reds and oranges – the colours of fire – are the warm colours, while blues and greys – the colours of ice and shadows – are the cool. In painting, as in other visual arts, the warm colours seem to come forward while the cool appear to recede, and if we bear this in mind in our work, a proper feeling of recession, or apparent depth, will be achieved. It is a matter of observation that the colours of the far distance are predominantly the blues and greys, and this is how we must therefore paint them. On very clear days, the greying of the distance is almost imperceptible and it then pays to exercise artistic licence and use a little more blue than we observe, in order to create a feeling of recession. The greying effect of distance is the result of viewing the far horizon through the intervening atmosphere which contains dust and, most of all, water vapour. The mistier the conditions, the greater this effect will be.

COMPLEMENTARY COLOURS

Let us now consider complementary colours. Just as realism in watercolour painting is enhanced by attention to colour temperature, so the use of complementary colours can heighten visual effect. In simple terms, these lie opposite each other on the colour wheel, for example red and green, yellow and violet, blue and orange. If you wish to discover a certain colour's complementary, this is what you do: paint a patch of that colour in the middle of a sheet of white paper, stare at it fixedly for about a minute and then switch your gaze to a small black dot in the middle of another sheet of paper. The complementary colour will then appear, a phenomenon sometimes termed the 'after image'.

Knowledge and understanding of complementary colours is useful in obtaining telling contrasts, and one sees many paintings in which full use has been made of their striking effect. A bright red figure in a predominantly green landscape is a frequently seen example of this. Vibrant

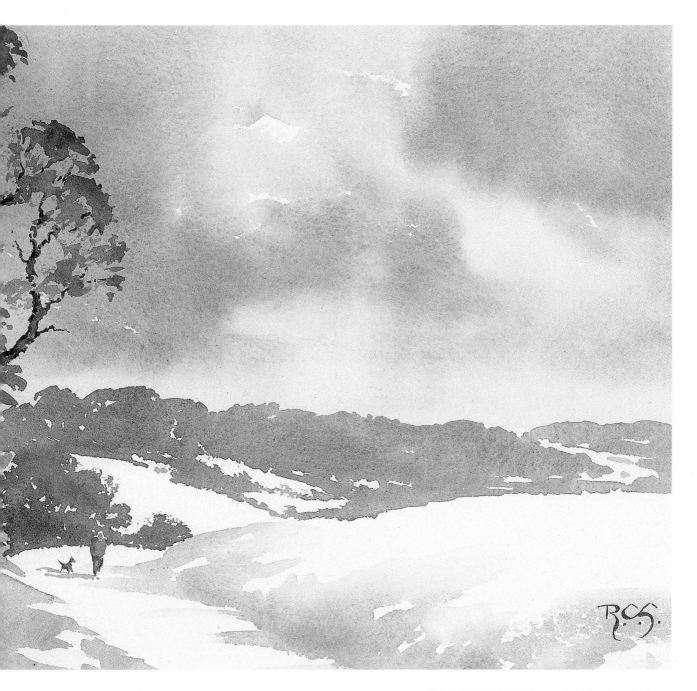

effects may be obtained by placing small areas of complementary colours side by side instead of mixing them, though this is a technique with more relevance to oil painting than to watercolour. Some of the French Impressionists, notably Seurat, extended and developed the technique which became known as *pointillism*.

USING COLOUR

Let us now get down to the practicalities of using colour. One of the first things we must do is rid ourselves of preconceived notions of colour – notions often inherited from our childhood. To young children, tree foliage is always bright green, tree trunks are uniformly chocolate brown, water is

SNOW OVER THE DOWNS
This winter scene illustrates several ways of reducing a landscape to a few quick and simple operations. For example, the sky – a rather heavy one to provide tonal contrast with the snow – was basically achieved by dropping a warm grey of ultramarine and light red into a pale base wash of raw sienna. In such liquid conditions the light red tends to separate, to give a warm edge to the clouds. The distant trees and hedges were

established in a single operation with a wash of ultramarine and light red. A little local colour was added here and there to give variety, and some extra water to lighten the tone on the right to aid recession. The foreground snow shadows were, once again, ultramarine and light red, in pale tones and softened in places with clear water. I used light red for the solitary figure to make it register against its predominantly green background.

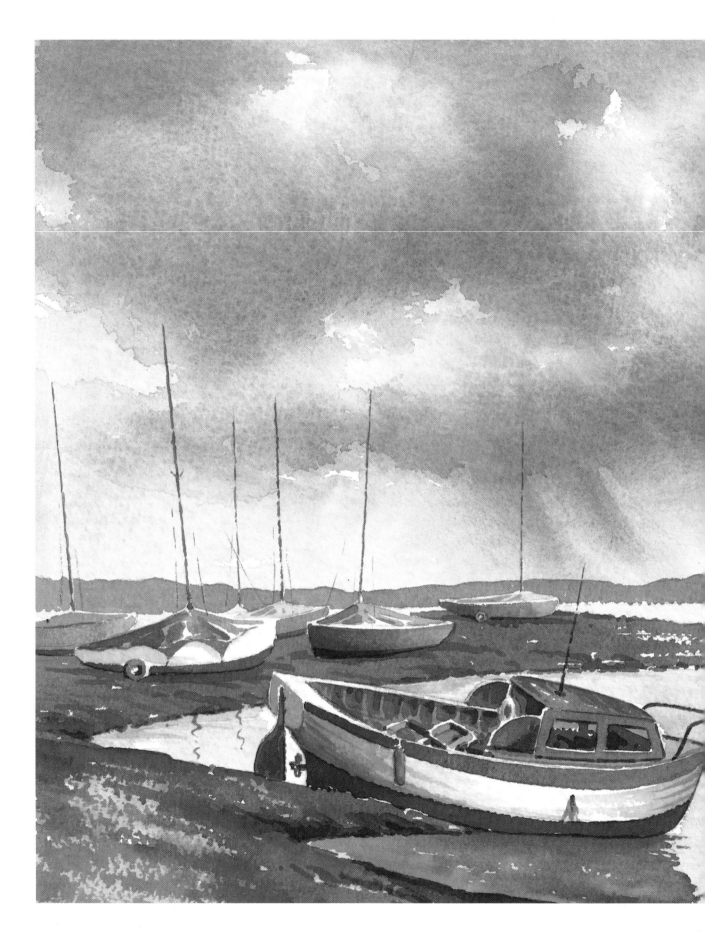

WATERCOLOUR FOR ALL

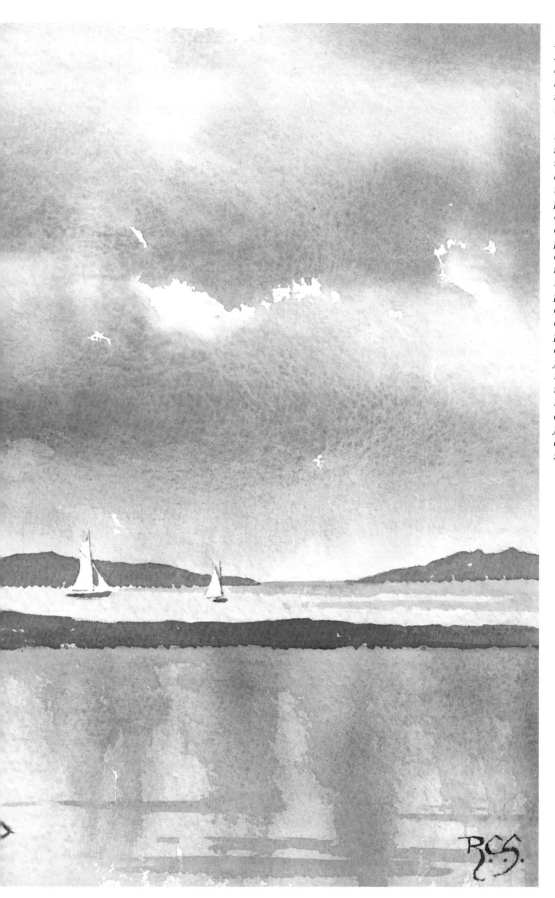

Here the gaily coloured sailing dinghies are contrasted with the solid lines of the fishing boat in the foreground. I seem to be using the word 'contrast' a great deal, but it is a vital ingredient in painting in all sorts of ways. Here are some additional examples: tonal contrast – the placing of lights against darks and vice versa; colour contrast – the placing of complementary colours in close proximity; textural contrast – the placing of rough surfaces against smooth. They can all be seen in this painting – the dark accents of the foreground boat against the pale water, the light red dinghies against their greenish setting and the rough foreground grass against the smooth surface of the water.

FRESH WATERCOLOURS: THE ULTIMATE AIM

The most important 'rule' of watercolour painting is to keep colours fresh and vibrant, and to avoid like the plague any hint of muddiness. Dullness and muddiness creep in when too many colours are combined in a wash, or when the remains of a wash of uncertain parentage are pressed into service. The beauty of watercolour is most apparent when the paper shines through a fresh and vibrant wash, and this beauty is all too easily lost by overworking or by the artist's use of muddy colours.

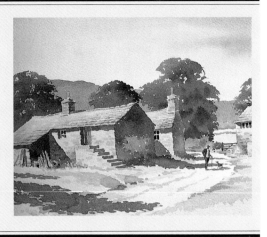

invariably bright blue and this is how they paint them. These early colour conventions are all too often carried unquestioningly into adult life and go some way to explaining the landscape paintings one frequently sees in which everything is an unrelieved green. Far better to ignore the colours we *expect* to see in our subject matter and look for what is *actually* there. If we look hard and analytically, it is often surprising what colours can be discovered and even though there may be only the merest hint of them, it may well pay to emphasise them, for this can give a painting more interest and character. This is particularly true of summer landscapes in which the colour green can be too dominant for comfort.

LIGHT

It is vital to remember that everything is influenced by the quality of the light. The light from a warm evening sky affects the colour of every object on which it falls and foreground foliage painted in cool green will look completely out of place. Some artists

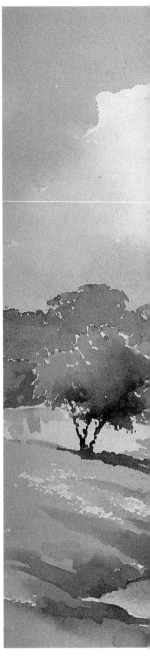

avoid this danger by carrying the warm sky wash down over the whole painting. The chips of that initial wash that remain untouched in various parts of the finished painting give a warmth and a unity to the whole. A similar type of unity can be achieved by using a tinted paper but, unless one keeps a large and varied stock, the chances of finding a sheet of the perfect colour are not very great. An overall wash, which varies to take account of the lighter colours which predominate in various parts of the painting, is another useful starting point and one which has the advantage of muting the rather intimidating white of the untouched paper.

It is not only that part of the landscape in full sunlight which is influenced by the sky – the shadows, too, are affected by the quality of the light and need careful study. If the sky is blue, the shadows will reflect that colour, and it is a bad mistake to indicate shadows with a wash of uniform grey. Warm light from nearby objects in full sunlight also have an appreciable effect and the lively →p.33

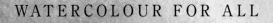

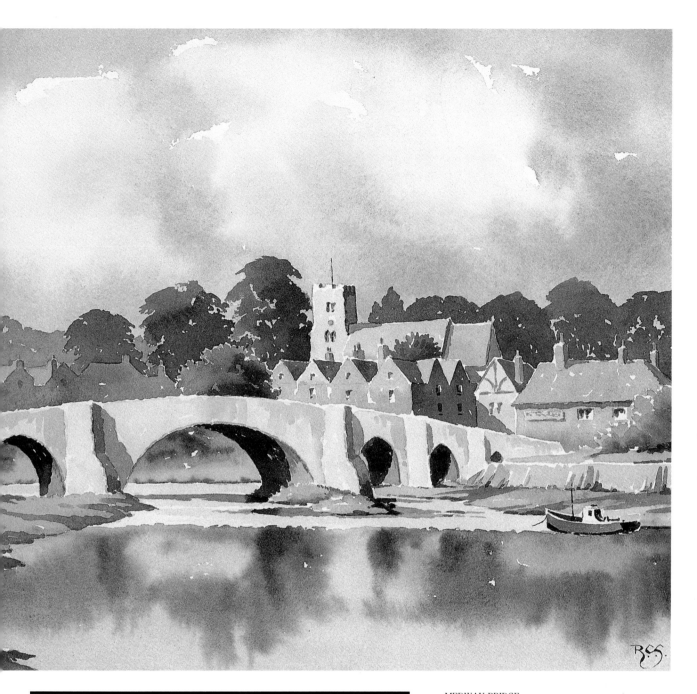

EXERCISES TO TRY

Here are a few experiments in colour you may care to try out:

1 Apply a horizontal wash to represent a field of fresh, sunlit grass (try raw sienna with a touch of Winsor blue).

2 Add a hedge and a few trees in deeper tones – perhaps various combinations of raw sienna, burnt sienna and Payne's grey.

3 Now add a small figure dressed in red, and note how it stands out against the green background.

4 Try mixing some subtle, warm browns, using only primary colours, and with these add some autumnal foliage to your watercolour sketch.

MEDWAY BRIDGE

This painting was built up with a series of flat, transparent washes which allowed the white of the paper to shine through. The church, the houses and the trees were all painted in this way and only in some nearer features, such as the bridge, the bushes and the foreground grass, did I permit myself any added texturing. Pale bands of disturbed water separate the scene above from its reflection, which is treated softly to provide contrast – a mirror image would have been altogether too complicated. The soft effect was obtained by adding vertical strokes of various colours to a wet base wash of pale grey.

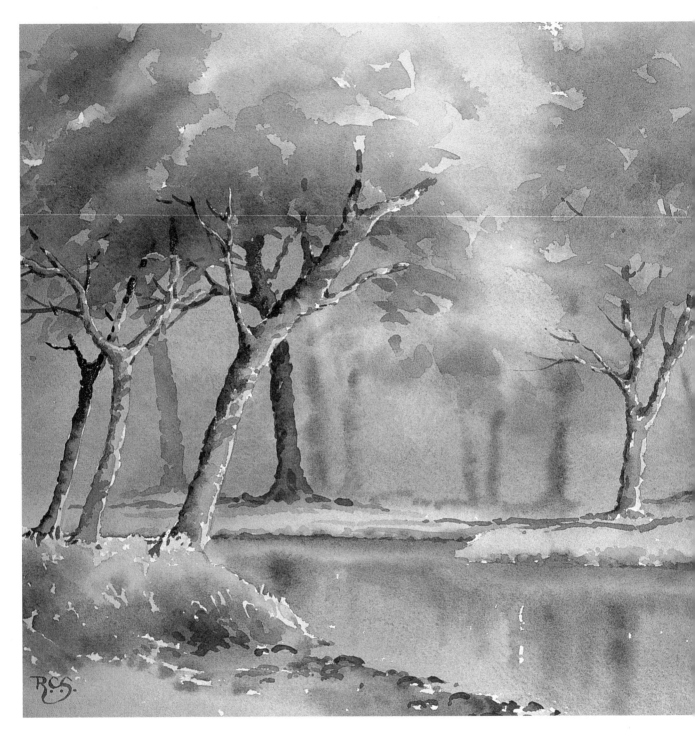

WOODLAND STREAM

An appreciation of colour is of particular importance to the watercolourist. The medium relies on subtlety and understatement rather than power and richness for its effect and this demands understanding, judgement and sensitivity on the part of the artist. At the same time there is no excuse for watercolours to be wishy-washy and the painter must be prepared to apply strong colour when the occasion demands.

Woods make fascinating subjects, particularly when there is some water on hand to provide reflections. Sadly, many inexperienced painters are deterred from having a go by the baffling complexity of leaves and twigs – they have not learnt the art of simplification or the power of suggestion. Here, all that detail has been resolved into broad areas of tone and colour, treated boldly and loosely, and only the tree trunks, which are fairly simple forms, have been given any detailed treatment.

Warmer colour has been introduced into this single wash impression of a tree in full leaf and the green no longer dominates.

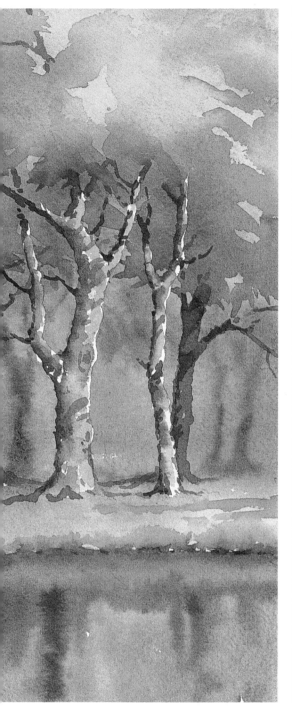

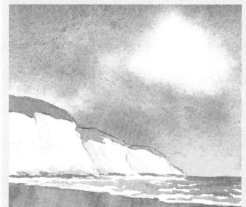

TONAL CONTRAST: the placing of lights against darks and vice versa. In this watercolour sketch the white cliffs contrast with the grey sky, while the shadowed expanse of sea on the right contrasts with the patch of luminous sky just above the horizon.

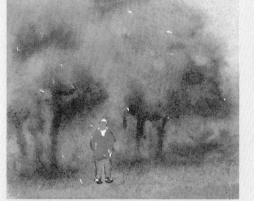

COLOUR CONTRAST: the placing of complementary colours in close proximity. Here the red of the jacket stands out boldly against the complementary green of the background. Notice that the blue/grey of the trousers provides no such contrast.

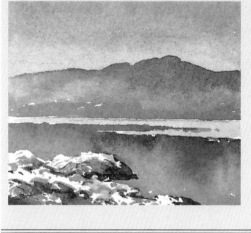

TEXTURAL CONTRAST: the placing of rough surfaces against smooth. The rough texture of the foreground rocks makes a useful foil for the expanse of smooth water.

treatment of reflected light will breathe life and beauty into shadowed areas.

TONE

Choice of colour and judgement of tone go hand in hand. In art, tone simply implies lightness or darkness and is not concerned with colour, as in popular usage. It is vitally important to get our tone values right and if we do, our paintings will still have form and meaning when photographed in black and white. A complicating factor is the disconcerting way watercolour has of drying several tones lighter. A wash that looks perfectly effective when first applied may well dry out weak and unconvincing, and due allowance has to be made for this.

Tonal contrast is an important ingredient in successful painting, and we should always be on the look-out for opportunities to place lights against darks and darks against lights. In the last analysis, sensitive appreciation of colour and sound judgement of tone will only come with careful observation, conscientious practice and experience, but the reward will be well worth the effort.

DUNSFOLD CHURCH

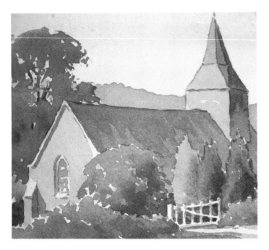

Thyis is one of those unspoiled hamlets where time seems to have stood still. It makes a delightful subject for the landscape artist, with its simple village church, weathered barn and sandy lane which leads the eye right into the centre of the composition. The soft colours of the afternoon sky add warmth to the old tile and brick of the cottage on the right, and these in turn lend warm reflected light to the shadowed side of the wooden barn. The North Downs form a pleasing back-drop of blue-grey while the deep tones of the late summer foliage contrast effectively with sunlit stone, timber and tile. The dappled shadow of a large tree off the painting to the left falls across the village green and adds a touch of interest to what would have been a rather empty foreground. It also helps to provide tonal balance to the painting.

Palette

raw sienna
light red
ultramarine
Payne's grey
burnt sienna
Winsor blue

STAGE 1

The octagonal spire of the little church needed careful drawing but the rest presented no problems.

The warm colour of the lower sky was a weak mixture of raw sienna and light red while the cloud shadows were ultramarine and light red, with rather more red towards the horizon. The clear sky was pale Winsor blue with a little added raw sienna. When I had prepared these washes I applied them as quickly as possible with large brushes. As the colour of the lower sky was very pale, there was no need to paint round the spire, the chimney or the trees. I might well have brought this warm wash down over the whole of the paper in the manner I describe in Chapter 7.

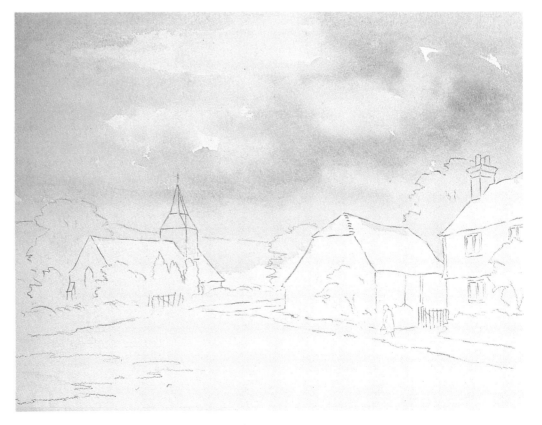

STAGE 2

Once again I tackled the trees at an early stage so that uninhibited brushwork might capture their broken outlines. I used washes of Payne's grey and raw sienna for the greenish trees, with added Payne's grey for the shaded areas. Plenty of burnt sienna was added for the russet-coloured trees and for the warmer parts of the hedge. The distant downs were then established using a flat wash of ultramarine with a little light red added and I had no difficulty in carrying this right up to the ragged outlines of the trees. A little raw sienna was added to the lower slopes.

The village green was a broken wash of Winsor blue and raw sienna, and when this was dry I added some texture with a large brush charged with a deeper mixture of the same colours. A wash of Payne's grey and raw sienna was applied with horizontal strokes to indicate the dappled shade on the left and the shadow cast by the line of the hedge.

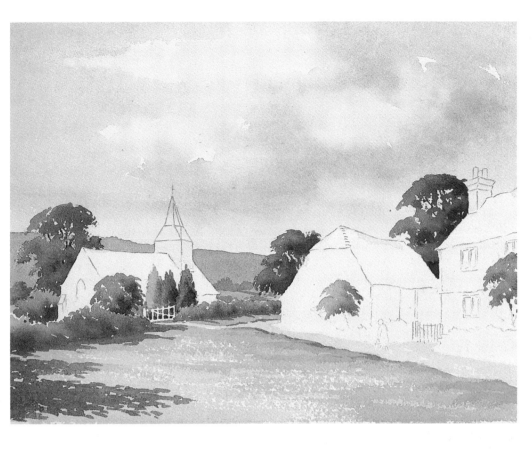

STAGE 3

The pale stonework of the little church was raw sienna, modified slightly with burnt sienna and ultramarine. Various combinations of burnt sienna and light red were used for the sunlit old tiles and brickwork, with a touch of green in the lower courses. Notice how these pale washes contrast with the deeper tones of the background trees and the shadowed elevations of the buildings. I painted the shaded side of the old barn in deep tones of ultramarine and light red with a little green

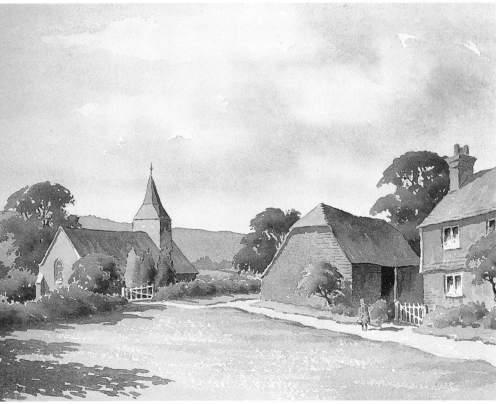

added at the base and took care to paint round the outline of the white gate, which makes a crisp accent against its dark background. I

finally added the small blue figure which appears to be moving, albeit slowly, into the centre of the painting.

3 Putting it in Perspective

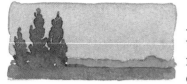

A fundamental problem which faces all painters is that of conveying in two dimensions a scene which exists in three. In early times artists had to rely entirely on observation and convention, and consequently the perspective of many of their paintings was by modern standards somewhat eccentric. In Renaissance times a system of linear perspective was evolved, based on geometric constructions, and an understanding of this ingenious yet basically simple theory enabled artists to solve their problems without difficulty. In practice, experienced artists still rely mainly on observation, for a drawing based entirely on geometry would appear somewhat mechanical and unnatural. At the same time, a knowledge of perspective construction makes it possible for them to check their work and iron out any difficulties that may arise.

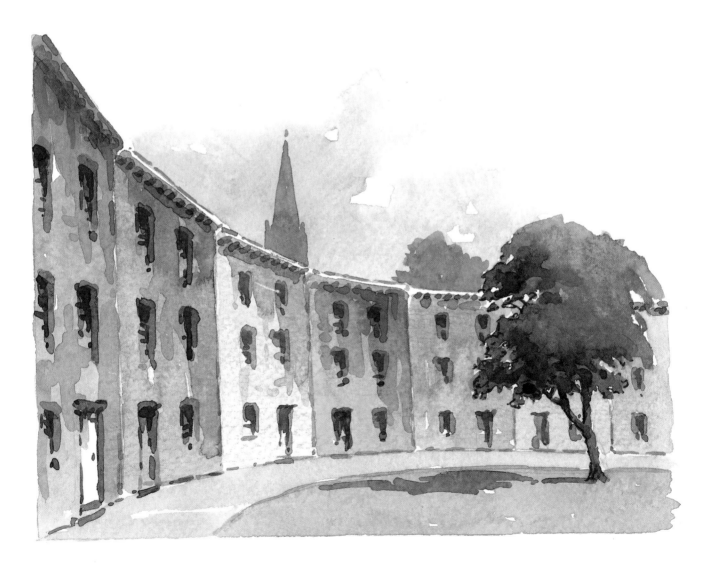

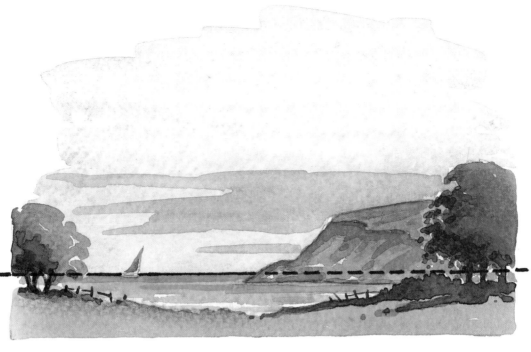

HORIZON   HORIZON

In this watercolour sketch the sea horizon coincides with the true horizon. In the right-hand half of the *illustration the true horizon is obscured by cliff and foliage. Here the difference between the* *true and the observed horizons is obvious, but this is not the case in much flatter terrains.*

LINEAR PERSPECTIVE

The theory of linear perspective is based upon the observable fact that objects of similar size appear to get smaller as they recede into the distance. Let us consider the case of a straight line of fencing posts, all of equal height, on a level plain. They will appear to get smaller as they recede until they become so small they disappear altogether. The lines connecting their extremities will be straight and will converge at a point on our eye level line, or horizon, known as a *vanishing point*. These lines are

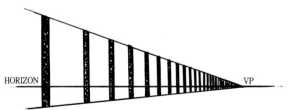

in fact parallel, since the posts are all of equal height, and yet the effect of perspective is to make them converge. Notice that one of these lines, that which joins the tops of the posts, is *above* eye level and slopes *down* to the horizon. The other, which is *below* eye level, slopes *up* to the horizon.

We must be quite clear what we mean by the term horizon, or eye-level line. Only in cases of a large expanse of calm water or a dead level plain will the observed horizon be

identical with the true horizon. In practice, mountains, hills, buildings, trees and so on obscure the true horizon, which then becomes an imaginary line.

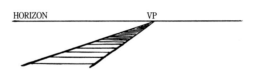

If we take the case of a straight run of railway track, also on a completely level plain, we will find the two lines converge, meeting at a vanishing point on the horizon, as in the figure above. From these models we can conclude that all lines that are parallel and on the same level plane will meet, when extended, at vanishing points on the horizon. Because the track is below eye level, the perspective lines slope up to the horizon. → *p.40*

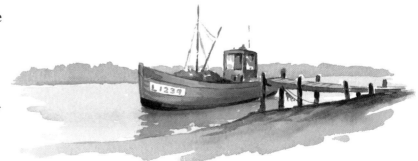

PUTTING IT IN PERSPECTIVE   37

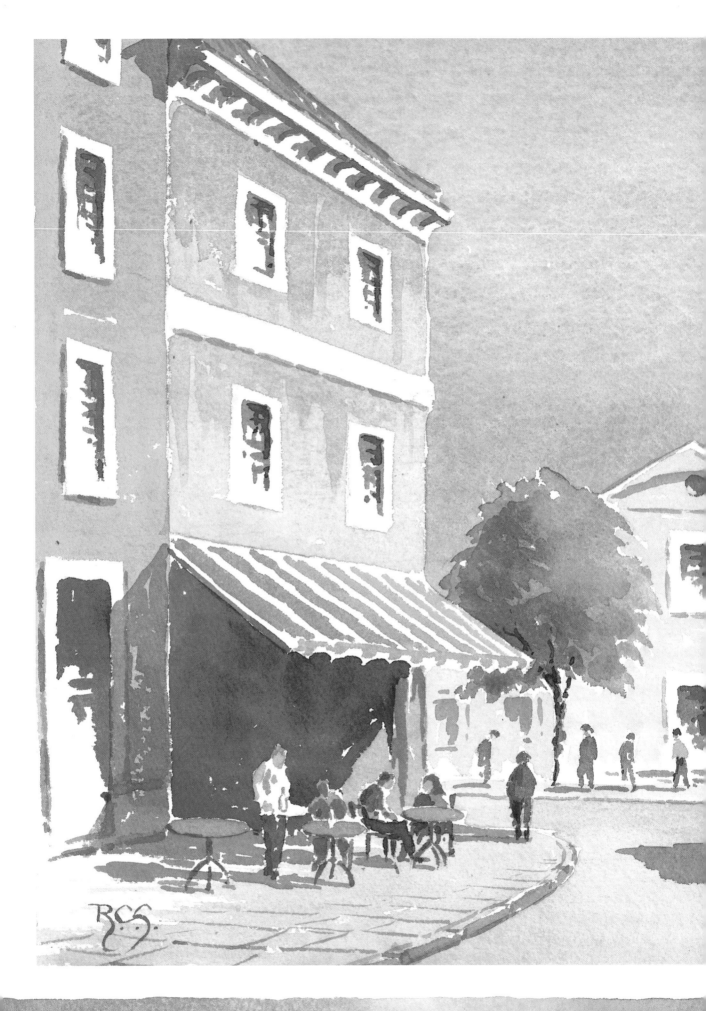

WATERCOLOUR FOR ALL

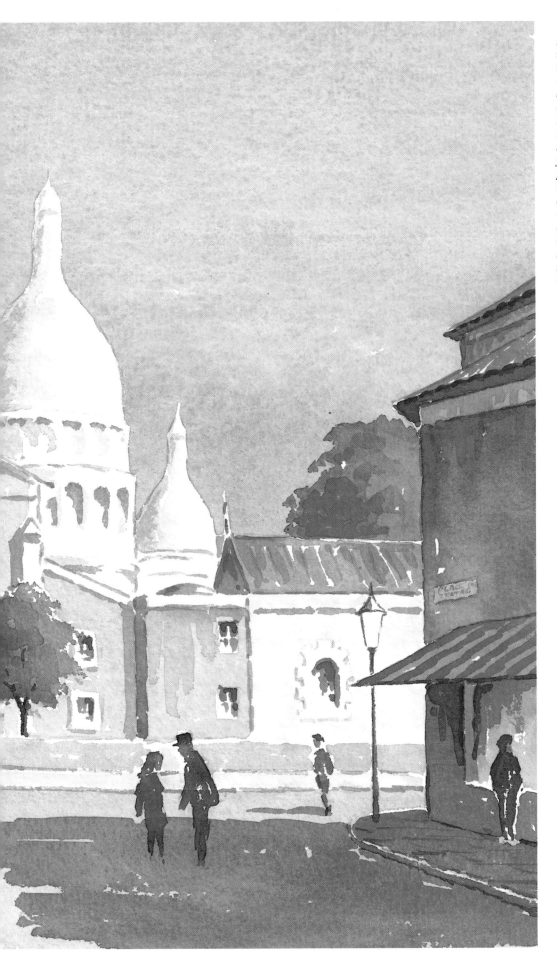

I was attracted by the manner in which the white limestone of the Sacré Cœur stood out against the deeper tone of the sky, and I was determined to preserve this contrast. The sunlit area of the stonework is just the white of the paper, and the sky is a mixture of ultramarine and light red. The wetness of the roadway enabled me to introduce more colour and interest into the foreground than if I had been faced with dry tarmacadam.

Pairs of parallels, set at an angle to each other, will all converge on the horizon, but at different vanishing points. A building, in the form of a solid rectangle, shown below, illustrates this point. Its perspective has been checked by extending, to the horizon, the pairs of parallels marking the tops and bottoms of the two side walls. If it is correct, these perspective lines will meet at two vanishing points on the horizon, as here.

Notice that the rectangular windows also conform to this construction. Another point to note is that these parallel lines appear much steeper in buildings that are close at hand than in those that are more distant. In the latter case, these lines will appear much more horizontal and will only meet at vanishing points well beyond the limits of the paper.

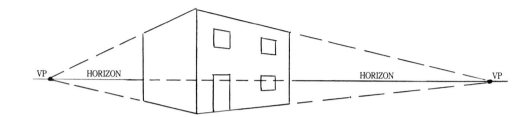

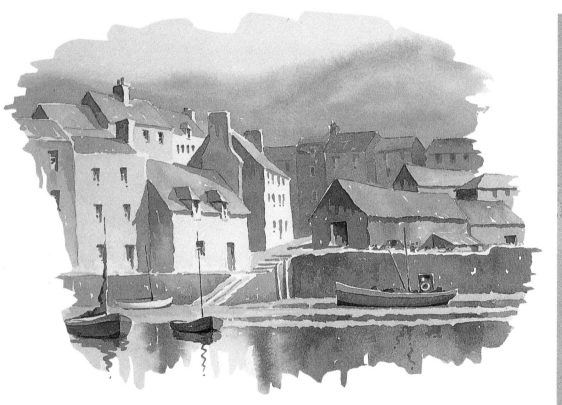

CORNISH HARBOUR

This vignetted watercolour sketch of a jumble of harbourside buildings called for a certain amount of care with perspective. When buildings are set at odd angles, they have different vanishing points. The lines of older buildings are often so irregular that the laws of perspective cannot be interpreted too literally.

Careful observation of light and shade will give your paintings of buildings additional interest as well as a three-dimensional quality and a feeling of solidity. Always look for colour in shadows and do not be content with an overall grey. If you look carefully at the shadows in this painting, you will see they contain a variety of colours and here and there evidence of warm, reflected light.

DERWENTWATER

The effects of aerial perspective are apparent in this watercolour sketch of the Lake District. The distant mountains are blue-grey in colour and this makes them recede. The foreground colours, by contrast, are warmer and much stronger and this brings them forward. Notice how the rain squall makes the hill behind appear even paler and mistier. Notice, too, how the far shore, and even the nearer shore, are virtually straight lines – the combined effects of distance and a low viewpoint.

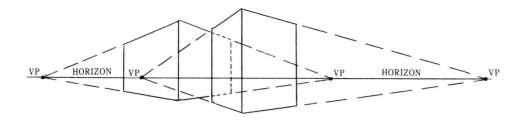

In the diagram above, the two buildings are set at different angles, so each house has a different pair of vanishing points, though these points are, of course, all still on the horizon or eye-level line. In all these constructions, the vertical lines remain vertical and are not affected by perspective. This is because our line of sight is level. Only if we are looking up or down will the vertical lines appear to converge.

It must be remembered that buildings have to be regular in shape and level in construction for this system of linear perspective to work. Older buildings, with very irregular and wayward lines, do not conform in this respect and then we have to rely on observation. There are other cases, too, where geometric construction cannot help us and here again the only answer is careful observation; there is, for example, no

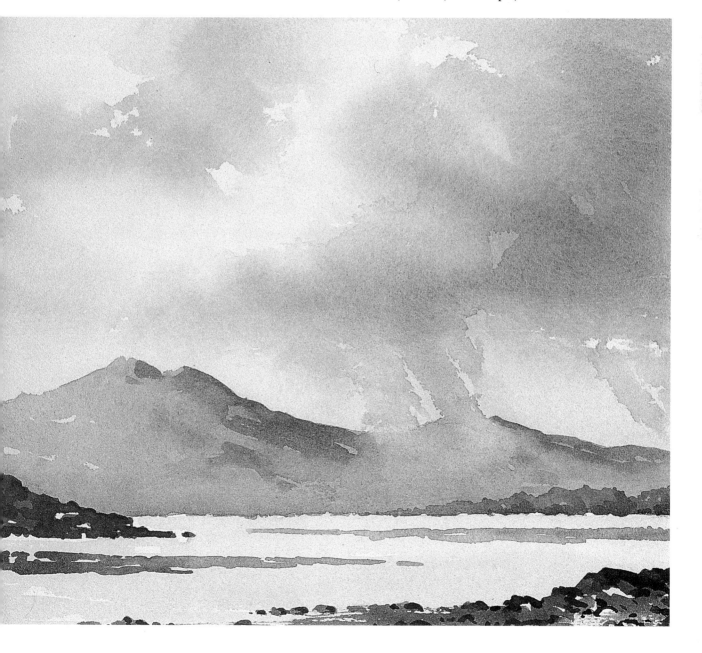

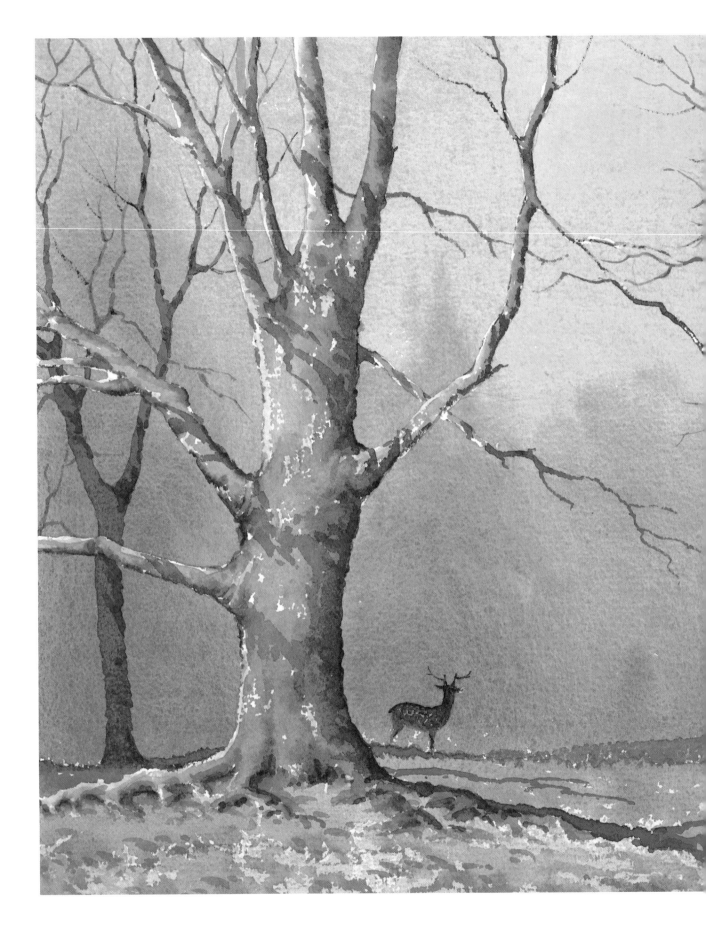

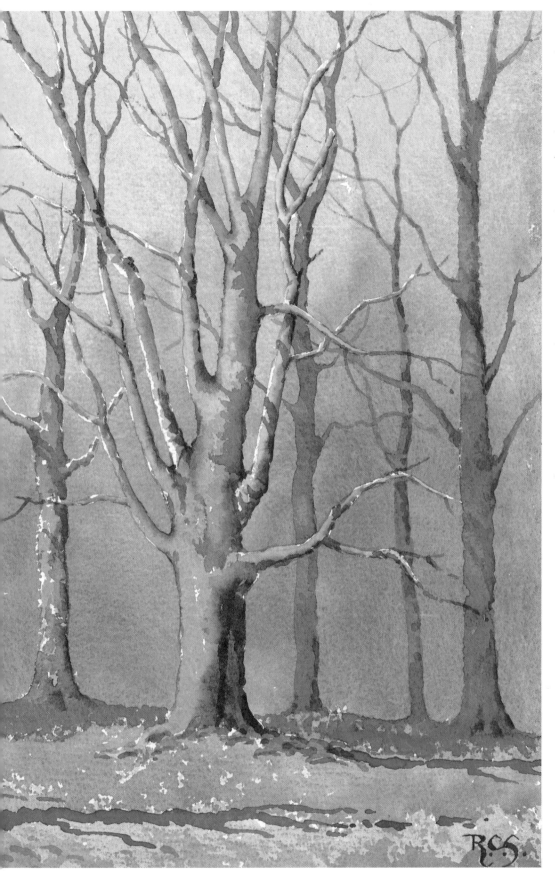

EVENING IN KNOLE PARK

The effects of aerial perspective are most apparent in misty conditions, when the softening effect of the atmosphere is accentuated. In this painting, the more distant tree forms are just vague shapes, almost lost in the warm evening mist. The nearer trees had to be crisply painted so that the contrasting treatment would create a feeling of recession. To obtain this effect, I painted the background in one loose operation, dropping warm greys into the wet sky wash to indicate the more distant trees but preserving the outlines of the nearer trees with liberal applications of masking fluid.

When everything was dry, I rubbed off the latex with my forefinger and painted the resulting white tree shapes with washes of greys and greens. The foreground went in next, with broken washes of burnt sienna and light red for the covering of dead leaves. The final touch was the young stag, taken from an old sketchbook, to provide scale and a focal point.

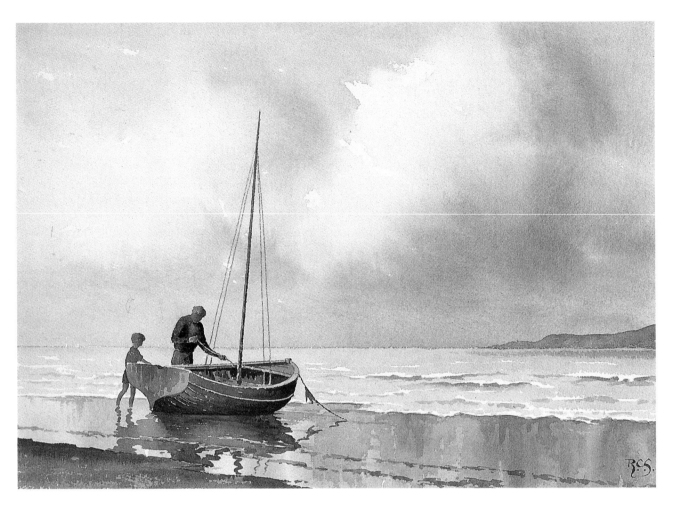

construction by which we can check the accuracy of our drawing of the lines formed by the banks of a river, but we will quickly realise that something is drastically wrong if the water in the painting appears to be flowing uphill!

AERIAL PERSPECTIVE

If our drawing is correct, our work will appear to have depth and objects will appear to recede convincingly into the distance. The effects of linear perspective will be strengthened by what is known as aerial perspective. The effects of aerial perspective stem from the fact that the atmosphere contains dust and water vapour, as we have already noted, and this softens the colours, the tones and the outlines of distant objects. Objects in the distance appear to lose their real colours and these are replaced by soft blues and greys, while tonal contrasts are much reduced or often lost altogether. This progressive softening and greying of objects as they recede into the distance contrasts with the warmer, stronger colours and far more definite tonal contrasts of the foreground. Aerial perspective reinforces the effects of linear perspective and diminishing scale in suggesting recession and depth. It is

achieved simply by the sensitive use of tone and colour.

When we have to rely upon our own observation and judgement, we can usually solve problems of proportion by measuring relative distances and size by the time-honoured method of holding a pencil at arm's length. Distances can then be measured and compared by moving the thumb along the pencil's length. A common fault is to give features such as distant fields or stretches of water too much depth. If we measure their depth and compare it with that of foreground features, this error will immediately become apparent. A related fault is that of giving a distant shoreline far too much vertical variation – the effect of distance will make it appear almost a straight line.

Never begin painting if you are unhappy with the perspective of your preliminary drawing. Paint has an uncomfortable habit of accentuating faults rather than obscuring them! Some artists deliberately distort perspective to create dramatic emphasis and this is perfectly legitimate. More questionable, to my mind, is the practice of violating the laws of perspective merely to convey a bogus naivety.

EBB TIDE, NORFOLK
On one visit to the Norfolk coast I was attracted by the reflection of the boat and the figures in the shallow water and wet sand. Notice how their strong, warm colours contrast with the soft grey of the distant headland, and how the straight line forming the base of that headland contrasts with the more wavy horizontals in the foreground.

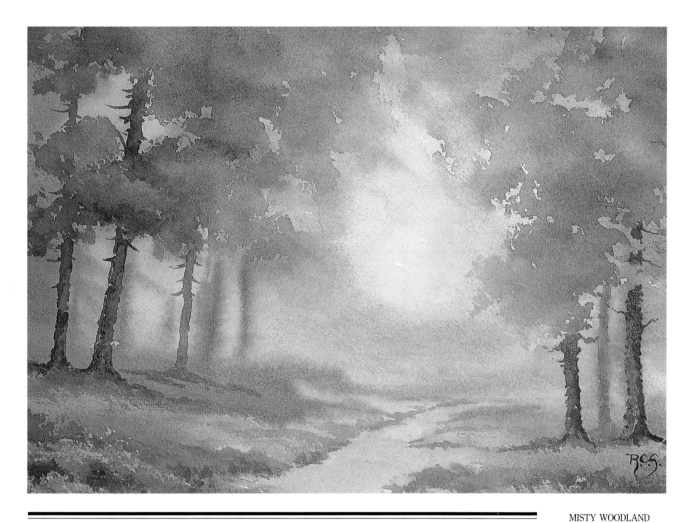

EXERCISES TO TRY

It is useful practice to draw a few solid rectangular shapes, with an indication of the true horizon, or eye-level line – and then test your accuracy in the manner described below:

1 Draw a rectangular building at an angle, showing two elevations, so that it is all *above* eye level.

2 Repeat, but with the whole building *below* eye level.

3 Repeat, with your eye level about half way up the rectangular building.

4 Check the accuracy of your drawings with the perspective construction. Did your vanishing points fall on the true horizon?

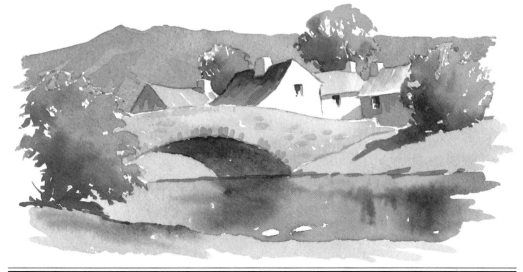

MISTY WOODLAND
In foggy or misty conditions, the effects of aerial perspective are much more apparent, as one would expect. In this study of misty woodland only the nearest features are at all hard edged, and the rest quickly lose definition as they recede.

This painting began with a pale wash of liquid raw sienna, plus a little light red, in the centre of the paper. To this, slightly deeper surrounding washes of grey-green were added. As this variegated wash began to dry a little, the forms of nearer trees were added, wet in wet, and as the paper was still damp, they were soft edged. Only when everything had dried did I put in the foreground trees, which of course retained their hard edges.

CALM ANCHORAGE

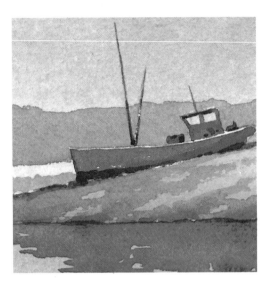

Coastal scenery has a great deal to offer the watercolourist, and sheltered inlets with boats at anchor have a particular appeal. In this scene the tumbledown fishermen's huts add to the attraction and, with their old brick and tile and rusty corrugated iron, are a source of rich, warm colour which contrasts effectively with the blue-grey of the distance, to create a strong feeling of recession. Although most of the tonal weight is on the right, the moored yacht on the left provides adequate balance. Notice how the distant shore is virtually a straight line.

Palette
raw sienna
light red
ultramarine
burnt sienna
Winsor blue

STAGE 1

The warm colours and soft cloud formations of the early evening sky appealed to me so I once again decided upon a low horizon, roughly one third of the way up the paper. There were many more boats than I have included, but I felt this simplification was justified, producing a balanced composition. The near spit of land and the distant line of low hills serve the useful purpose of linking the various boat shapes together, while the vertical masts connect the planes of sea, land and sky. In a composition such as this, in which these elements form three horizontal bands across the paper, masts can perform a useful connective function.

Once I was satisfied with the lines of my sketch, I mixed up four washes for the sky: very dilute raw sienna warmed with light red for the sunlit areas of

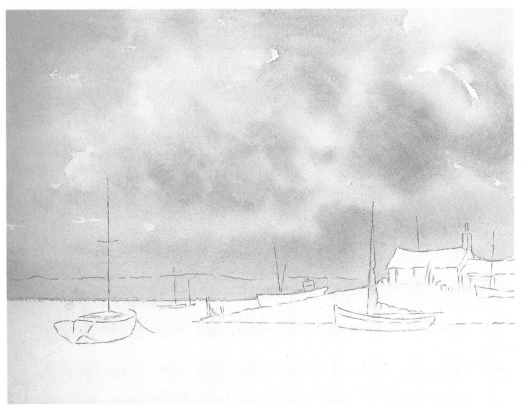

cloud; two greys, a warm and a cool (from mixing ultramarine and light red in different proportions) for the cloud shadows; and pale

Winsor blue for the area of clear sky. I applied these washes quickly and directly with large brushes. A few odd chinks of white paper

remained untouched, but I made no attempt to tidy them up as I felt they prevented the sky from appearing too smooth and bland I

brought the warm grey of the lower sky down over the distant hills but painted round the huts on the right.

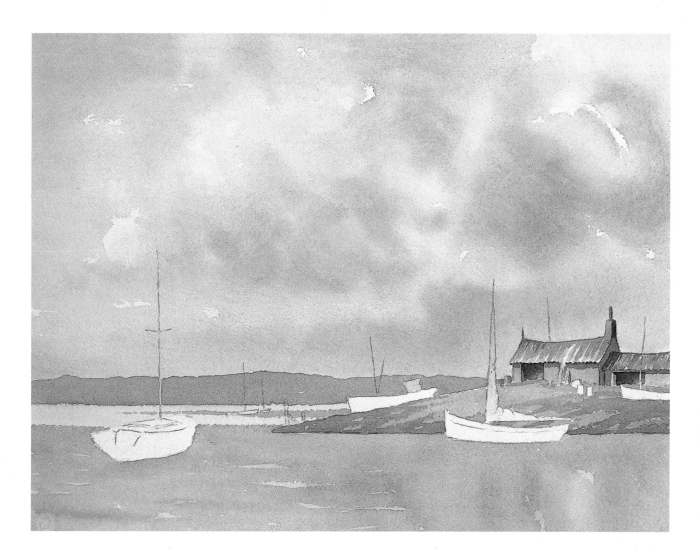

STAGE 2

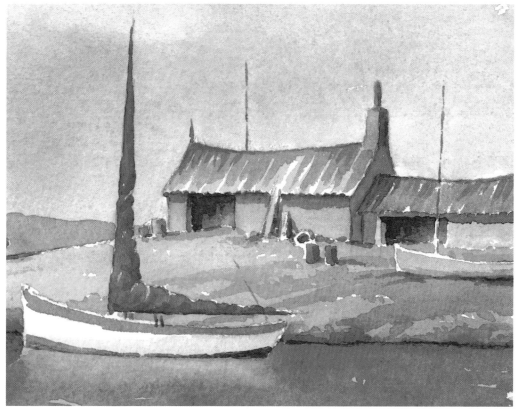

Once the sky had dried, I applied a pale wash of ultramarine and light red to represent the distant estuary and a deeper wash of the same colours for the far shore and its thin line of reflection below. The nearer, smoother water was a warm grey with some soft wet in wet vertical and horizontal additions in cooler grey. The fishermen's huts went in next in warm tones, mainly burnt sienna and light red, to represent brick, tile and rusty corrugated iron. Notice how the brush strokes follow the slope of the roofs. The rough grass was a pale mixture of raw and burnt sienna plus a little ultramarine, and when it was dry I added a texturing wash of the same colours.

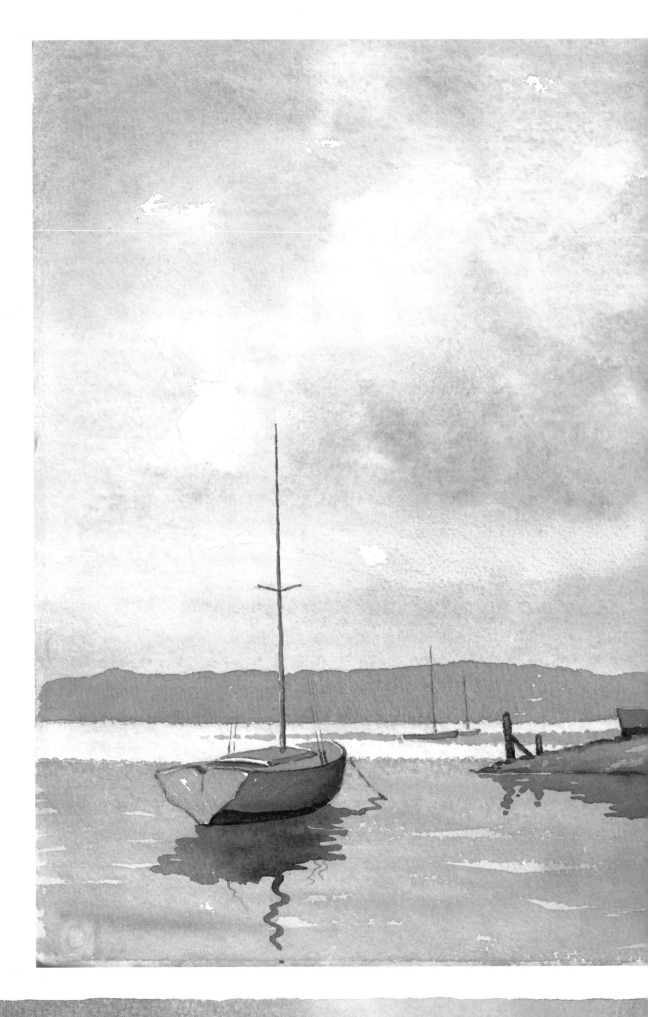

WATERCOLOUR FOR ALL

I now started painting the boats in a variety of tones and colours, the moored yacht on the left in fairly deep colour to provide tonal balance, and the boat just below the hut in pale tones to help it register against its rather darker background. When all this detail was complete, I prepared pools of colour for the reflections which I planned to tackle in single washes, varying the colour as I went. The colours corresponded with those of the objects above but were generally deeper in tone, with a green tinge which echoed the local colour of the water. In painting reflections of this type, remember that the distant ripples are more foreshortened than the nearer ones due to the effect of perspective.

PUTTING IT IN PERSPECTIVE

4 Composition and Balance

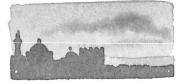

Howorever skilled one's watercolour technique may be, the resulting painting can never be satisfactory if the composition is faulty. The vital importance of good composition is universally recognised and yet it is a goal that many competent painters find hard to achieve. Let us consider for a moment just what composition is and try to strip away some of the accumulated mystique.

Quite simply, composition is the arrangement of the elements of a painting on paper or canvas. Good composition results when these elements are arranged in a harmonious and pleasing manner. People vary widely in their ability to recognise or formulate good composition, but in my experience most people who are attracted to art have a natural feeling for form and balance, and, if they are encouraged and well taught, soon begin to develop a sound sense of design.

THE POSITIVE APPROACH TO COMPOSITION

There are two approaches to the study of composition, one positive and one negative, and both have their value. The positive approach is naturally more concerned with what to aim at rather than what to avoid and this we shall deal with first. Let us begin by considering rather more fully what we mean by *good composition*; it is the pleasing and harmonious arrangement of the shapes, the colours and the tones of a painting within the rectangle of the paper or canvas. If we look at a painting, concentrating on form and trying to ignore subject matter, we can begin to see it as a design rather than a picture, an arrangement of shapes and colours that together make a pattern. Patterns can be pleasing and satisfying or the reverse, or, perhaps, something not very striking between the two extremes. The first step in improving the composition of our work is to recognise that the arrangement of the elements on our paper needs far more care and consideration than it normally receives. Thus we need to give much more thought to what has been termed 'picture organisation'.

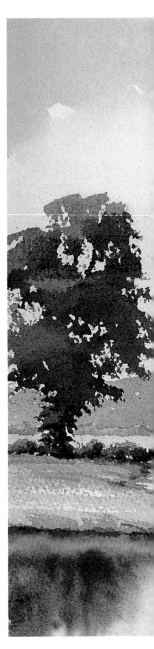

WEALDEN FARM
In this painting, the farm buildings overlap and so relate to one another, while the deep-toned trees behind provide useful contrast. The variety of building materials adds to the interest, and old brick and tile, painted and rusty corrugated iron all provide opportunities for using rich colour. The winding farm track leads the eye into the painting, and the deep-toned tree on the left and its equally deep reflection in the farm pond help to balance the composition.

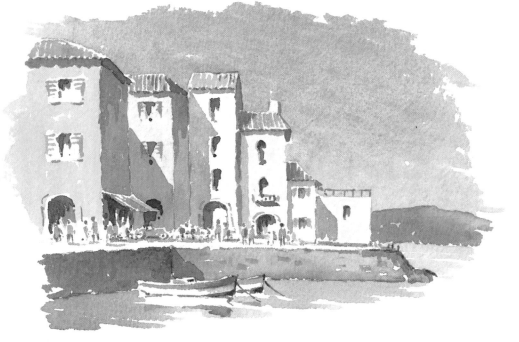

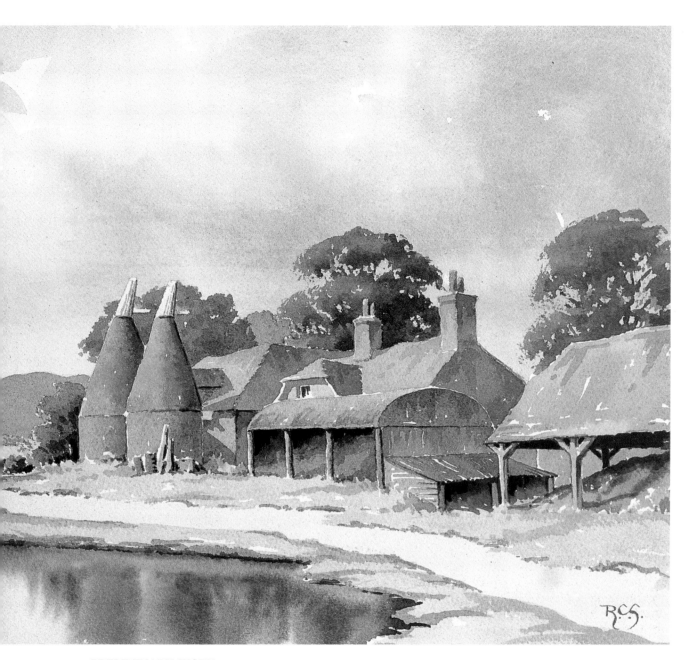

PRELIMINARY WORK

Design is easier to assess if it can be considered without the complicating intrusion of subject matter, and this consideration is best applied when one's thoughts are still in a fairly fluid state – it is much too late once the drawing is complete and the painting has begun.

I always make several rough sketches of my subject from various angles, using a viewfinder (*see* page 65), in an attempt to discover the most suitable vantage point and the most attractive arrangement of the elements of that subject. This is the stage at which to think about design. One way to concentrate attention on the pattern of the chosen sketch is to outline in black, perhaps with a broad-tipped marker pen, the various elements in that sketch, remembering that

negative shapes (ie the shapes *between* objects) are just as important as positive ones (ie the shape of the objects themselves). These elements will all vary in size, shape and tone and the resulting pattern will be much easier to assess in terms of balance and harmony if we regard it simply *as* a pattern. It would be more helpful still if the rough lay-out had colour as well; I know several artists who add both colour and tone to their rough work to help them in their search for good composition. However, I find a great deal can be learnt from black and white alone. If the bold design that emerges has balance and harmony, these qualities will be apparent in the finished painting, even though in a less obvious form. If, on the other hand, the pattern is less pleasing and lacks balance, that is the time to reassess its

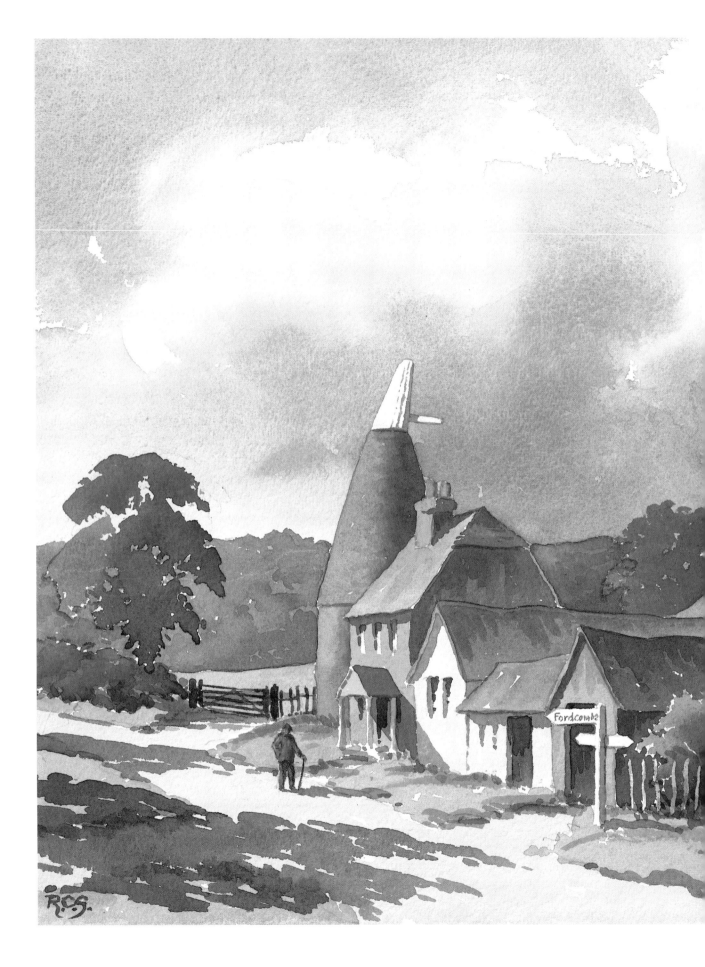

WATERCOLOUR FOR ALL

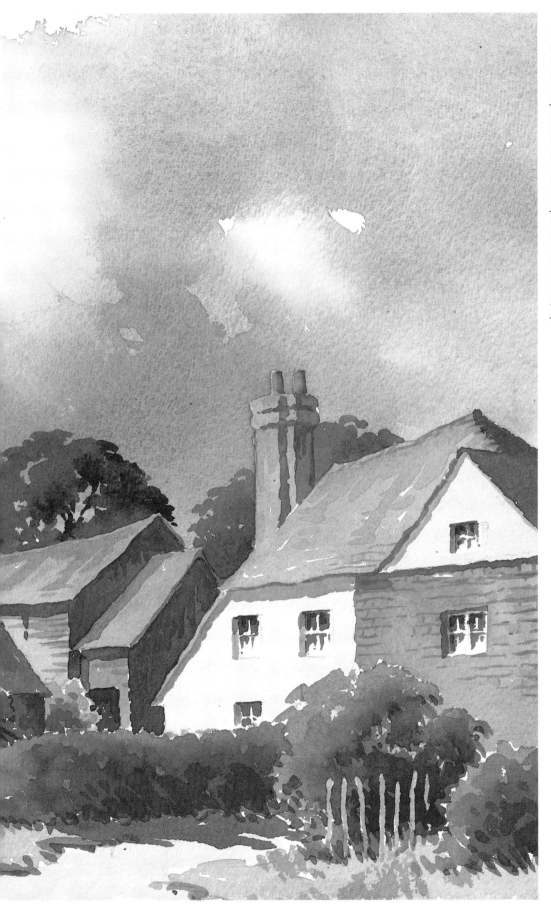

This is another example of a group of farm buildings with a variety of shapes, colours and textures combining to form a pleasing, rather than a perfect, composition. There is an attractive overlap of shapes and plenty of tonal contrast, but there is, unfortunately, nothing to stop the eye following the line of road straight off the painting to the left. A larger sheet of paper would have made possible the inclusion of a group of trees which could have performed that useful function and acted as a 'stop'.

COMPOSITION AND BALANCE

arrangement and organisation. A little experimenting and trial-and-error at this stage is well worth the effort. The urge to get on with the painting is strong, but it must be firmly resisted until we are certain our composition is both pleasing and balanced.

USING THE GOLDEN MEAN

In the past, when many artists worked exclusively in the studio, it was common practice to base compositions upon definite geometric forms, and although the underlying constructions were usually softened and modified during the painting process, the basic framework remained – as can be seen in many of the great paintings of the past.

One development of this geometric approach to composition was the discovery of what became known as the divine proportion of the golden mean, or section. This concept, originally invented by the Athenian geometrician Euclid, was an attempt to divide a line in an aesthetically perfect manner. Today artists rarely plan their work on a rigid Euclidean framework, but it is true that many of the more satisfying compositions of the masters have significant points close to the Golden Mean, otherwise known as the Golden Section.

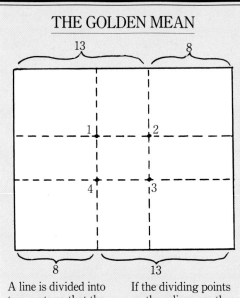

THE GOLDEN MEAN

A line is divided into two parts so that the ratio of the smaller to the larger is equal to the ratio of the larger to the whole line. In practice this means dividing the line in the ratio of approximately 8 to 13. If the lines forming the sides of a rectangle are divided in this ratio, the construction will appear as above.

If the dividing points on these lines are then joined to corresponding points on the opposite sides of the rectangle, their intersections, at points 1, 2, 3 and 4 in the diagram, are held to be of special significance, and the theory states that important points in the composition should be placed at or close to them.

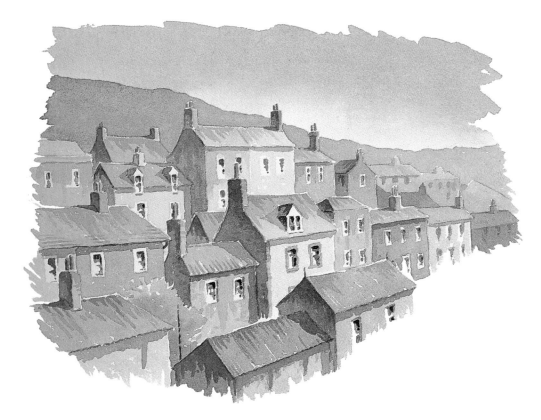

WELSH TOWNSCAPE
Even when the buildings in a painting are arranged in straight lines and are all facing in the same direction, variety of form and diversity of colour in the buildings themselves can combine to produce interesting patterns. In this painting, the high viewpoint aids the composition and the range of colours and tones adds a certain interest.

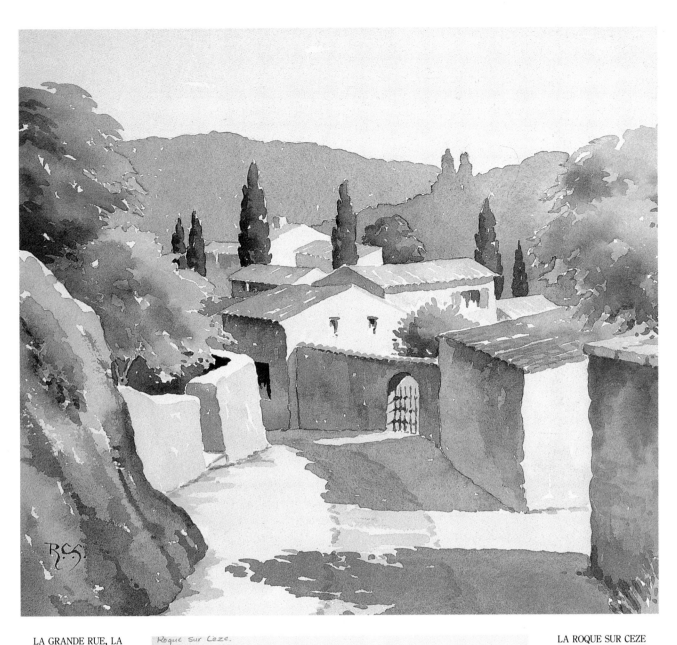

LA GRANDE RUE, LA ROQUE

The jumble of Roman-tiled buildings in this delightful Provençal hill village offers the artist a wealth of attractive compositions. Here, the sunlit and shadowed elevations of the buildings produce an interesting pattern, while the lateral shadows help to break up the rather large expanse of foreground road. The vertical forms of the cypress trees contrast pleasantly with the mainly horizontal lines of the tiled roofs.

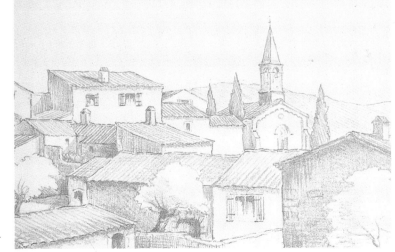

Roque sur Ceze.

LA ROQUE SUR CEZE

This panorama of jumbled, Roman-tiled roofs was the view from a bathroom window. I sketched it quickly with a 2B pencil and made the most of the verticals of the belfry and cypress trees. I later used this sketch as the basis for a watercolour in which one of my objects was to do justice to the rich colours of the tiles and the warm, reflected light in the shadows.

THE NEGATIVE APPROACH
TO COMPOSITION

The negative approach to the formulation of good composition naturally hinges on things to avoid and some artists find a list of unambiguous 'don'ts' of greater help than the more nebulous precepts of the positive approach.

What, then, should we try to avoid in our quest for sound composition? A number of examples of poor arrangement are illustrated in the left-hand column below, with my suggested corrections on the right. There are many ways in which we can do violence to the laws of composition, but those I have shown seem to occur most frequently. Perhaps I should not use the term 'laws' in this context, for these precepts do not have the force of the ten commandments. I can think of many successful paintings which breach the rules, but there is nearly always a good reason for this and it still makes good sense to observe them whenever possible.

Faults often creep in if we begin to apply paint before fully working out our composition, so do not let your keenness to start painting tempt you to cut corners!

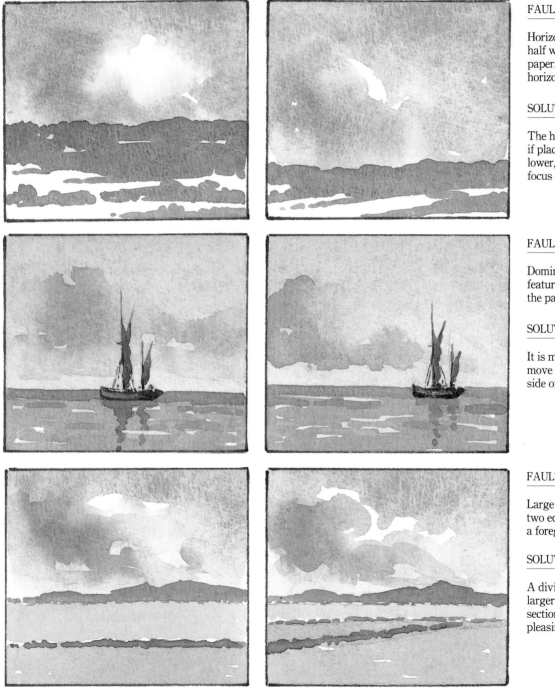

FAULT

Horizontal line placed half way down the paper; this is often the horizon.

SOLUTION

The horizon looks better if placed either higher or lower, depending on the focus of interest.

FAULT

Dominant vertical feature half way across the paper.

SOLUTION

It is much better to move the object to one side of the centre.

FAULT

Large area divided into two equal strips, such as a foreground field.

SOLUTION

A division which creates larger and smaller sections is more pleasing to the eye.

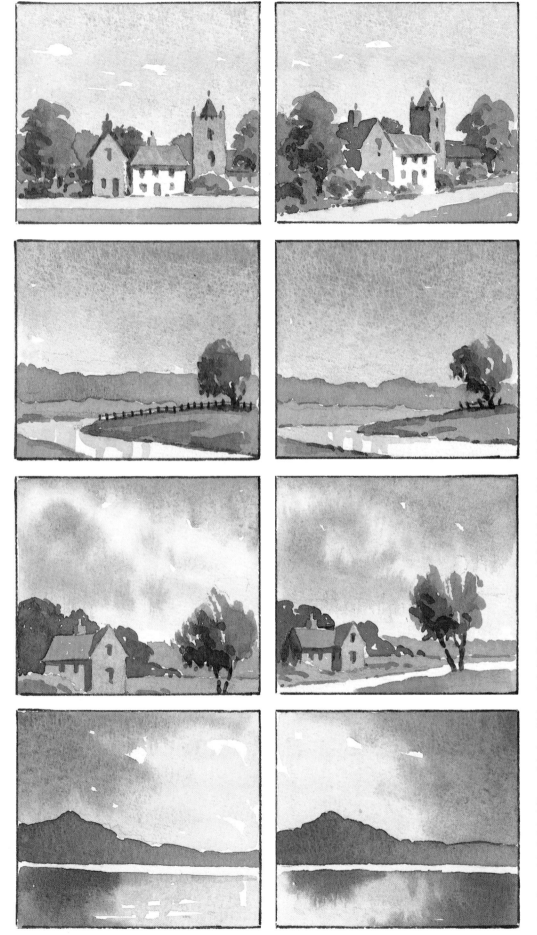

FAULT

Objects appear to be strung out in a straight line, without a connecting link.

SOLUTION

Adopt a viewpoint from which there is some overlapping and some relationship between individual objects.

FAULT

A dominant line emanating precisely from the corner of a painting.

SOLUTION

Revise the composition so that important lines no longer originate in the corner of the painting. Modify lines of excessively regular fencing.

FAULT

Important feature (for example, a building) positioned so that it appears to be resting on the bottom margin of the paper.

SOLUTION

Simply plan ahead to avoid this situation arising – place the object some way above the bottom.

FAULT

All the tonal weight appears on one side of the painting.

SOLUTION

If the deep tones all occur naturally to one side of the composition, balance them by including some tonal weight on the opposite side – for instance heavy cloud shadows.

COMPOSITION AND BALANCE

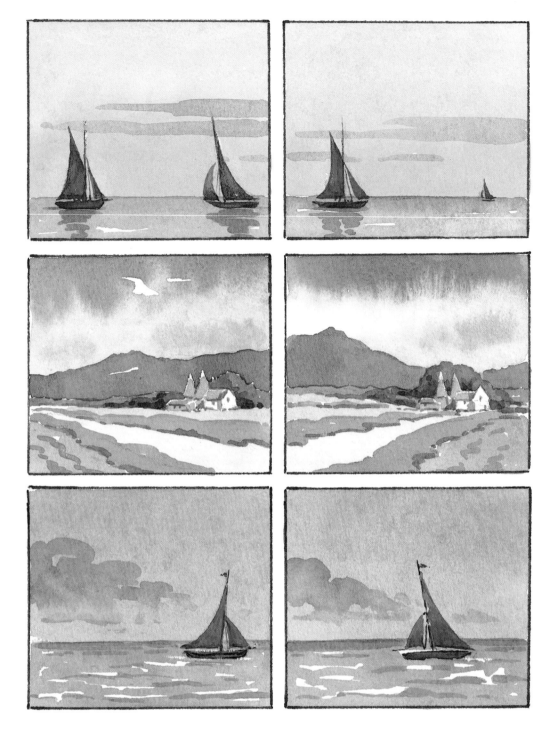

FAULT

Two competing centres of interest.

SOLUTION

Concentrate attention on one centre of interest, and sacrifice anything else that might detract from it.

FAULT

The viewer's eye is drawn away from the centre of interest by the compositional lines created.

SOLUTION

Arrange the painting so that all elements draw the eye towards the centre of interest.

FAULT

The viewer's eye is drawn off the paper, here by the sailing boat.

SOLUTION

Turn the boat around so that it sails into the picture!

Quite a lot to remember! The danger is that the careful observation of so many rules may lead to dull, conventional compositions and this is just as bad as employing compositional ploys that are obvious and totally lacking in subtlety. In striving to achieve balance, do not overdo it and end up with too much symmetry. Remember that rules *can* be broken, but only if there is good reason to do so. Above all, in aiming for harmony and balance, do not sacrifice interest and impact.

Now try out this 'negative' approach for yourself. Cover the captions opposite, and see how many compositional faults you can find in the top painting. Then look to see how many were present. The lower painting demonstrates how an artist can improve the same view by applying a few basic rules of composition. Have a close look at what I have done before going on to try out a few compositional exercises in practice.

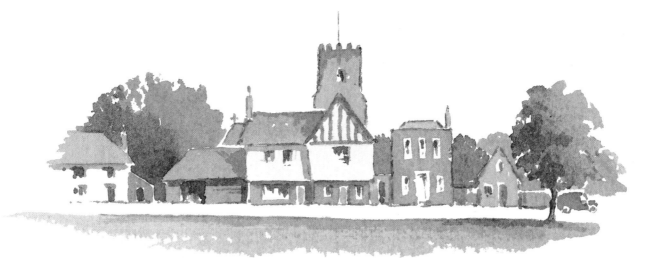

(Above)
There are several compositional shortcomings in this sketch of a village street. The flat, four-square view lacks interest and results in the buildings being strung out in a straight line. The strong vertical of the church tower is at the very centre of the group, exactly behind the half-timbered gable. The pale, unbroken strip of the foreshortened road cuts right through the composition and carries the eye off the paper at either end.

(Below)
Here the oblique viewpoint results in a more pleasing arrangement, with the buildings overlapping one another and so forming more positive relationships. We can see the shadowed sides of several houses and so there is more opportunity for tonal contrast. The church tower has been moved to the left and is balanced by the tree on the right, which also stops the eye sliding off the paper at that point. The road is no longer a straight strip of uniform width and it is broken by the shadow of the tree. Even the red mail van is moving into the picture instead of out of it.

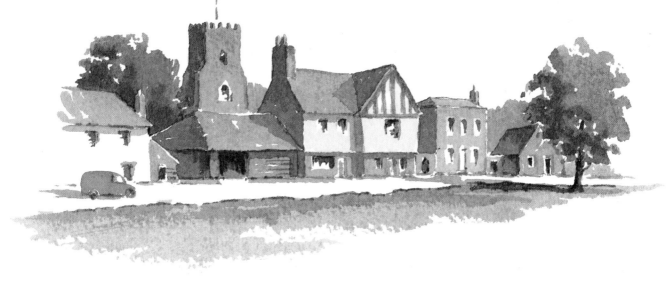

EXERCISES TO TRY

Using a 2B or a 4B pencil, test your natural skill at composing a pleasing and balanced arrangement:

1 Make a quick sketch of a group of buildings and trees in your neighbourhood.

2 Are you satisfied with the composition? If not, list any compositional faults you can spot.

3 Repeat the critical process, this time using the list of ten things to avoid mentioned on pages 56–58. Have any more faults come to light?

4 Re-draw your subject, correcting any faults in your sketch.

COTTAGES AT FILKINS

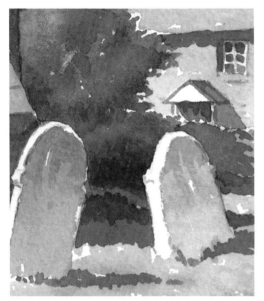

The unplanned and unregulated growth of old villages often resulted in attractive groupings and pleasing natural compositions and this is particularly true of the Cotswold area. This village group, clustering round its medieval church, is a delightful example and the varying angles and asymmetrical lines of the old stone cottages produce a pleasing pattern, which is helped by the gravestones and bushes in the foreground and the darker-toned trees in the background. The church porch is in shadow and is balanced by the shaded sides of the cottages on the right while the gravestones, some in sunlight and some in shadow, add interest to the foreground.

I made several quick sketches from various angles and each had its advantages, but I finally decided that this view produced the most pleasant composition.

Palette
raw sienna
light red
ultramarine
Payne's grey
burnt sienna
Winsor blue

STAGE 1

It was a warm afternoon in late September and the cloudless sky simply required a variegated wash of pale Winsor blue with a little raw sienna lower down. I sometimes introduce imaginary clouds if I feel the sky needs extra interest, but here there was a lot of detail in the scene below and a very simple sky made a pleasing contrast. I prepared two washes, one of Winsor blue, the other of raw sienna. With a 1in (2.5cm) flat brush I began applying the blue at the top, as described above, and about halfway down started dipping the brush in the raw sienna wash, producing a gentle gradation of colour. There was still some blue in the lower sky, as intended. I had no difficulty in painting round the outlines of the various chimneys, but if you find this a problem they could easily be preserved with the aid of masking fluid.

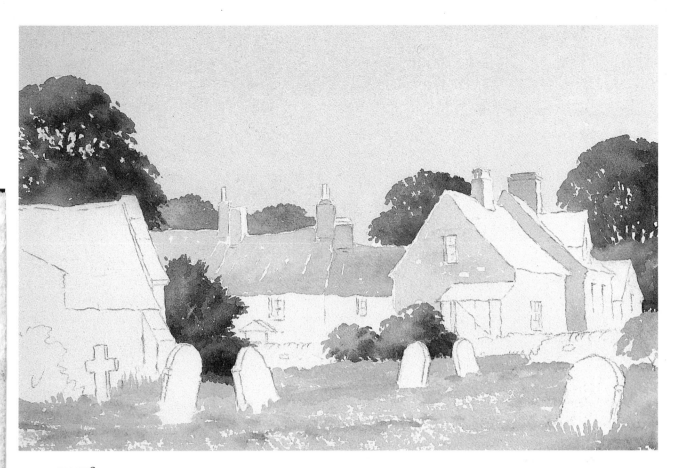

STAGE 2

The Cotswold stone walls and tiles were a pale honey colour which called for a subtle mixture of raw and burnt sienna, light red and ultramarine. Their tone was only a little deeper than that of the sky, but this did not matter as there was plenty of deep-toned foliage behind them. The more distant trees were blue-grey with just a hint of warmth, but two of the nearer ones were distinctly autumnal in colouring and for these I used raw and burnt sienna and Payne's grey.

The greener, right hand tree was just raw sienna and Payne's grey. I applied broken washes of these colours, using the side of the brush in order to take full advantage of the roughness of the paper, and added deeper tone, wet in wet, on their shadowed sides. The foreground bushes were tackled in a similar manner, but the yew contained a higher proportion of Payne's grey. The foreground grass was a broken wash of Winsor blue and raw sienna.

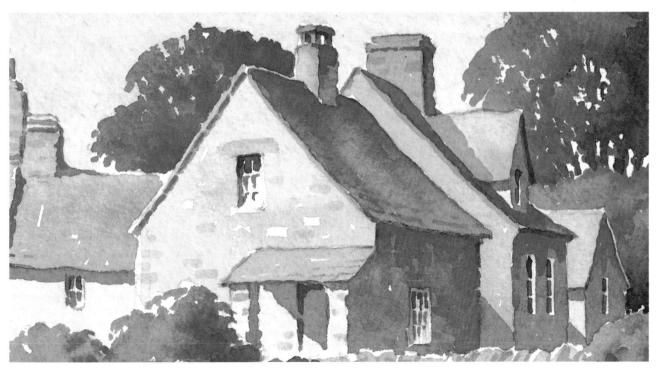

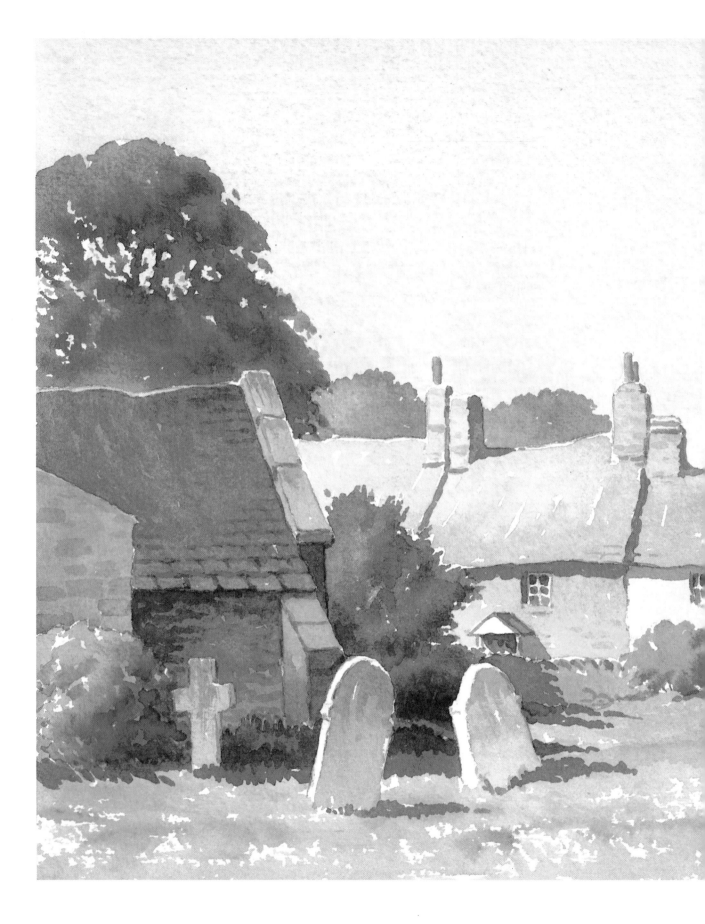

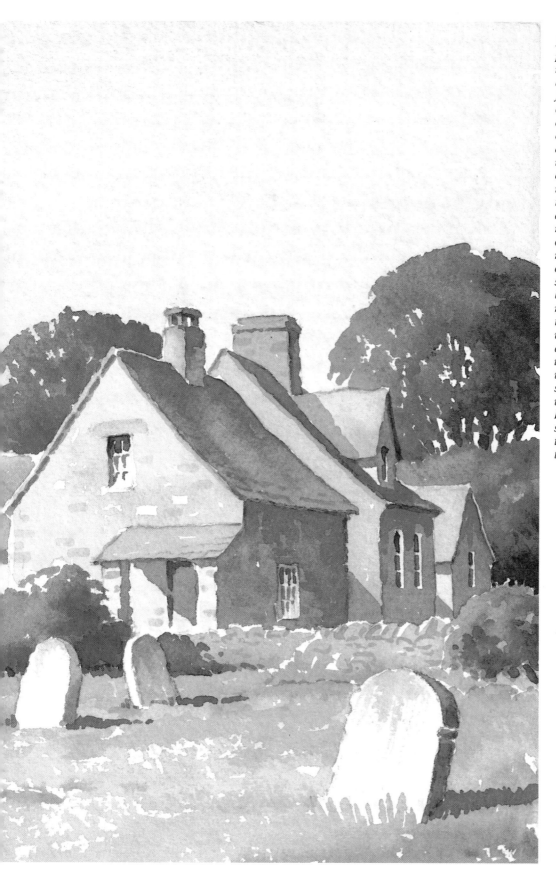

My next step was to paint in the cottage walls in a variety of pale tones and add deeper accents for the shadows cast by chimneys, roofs and eaves. The shaded sides of the cottages and the church porch on the left went in next in washes of ultramarine and light red, modified here and there with burnt sienna and green. I added a few random stones to the cottage walls and the merest suggestion of the courses of the stone slates. The church porch, being nearer, received rather more detail. I treated the gravestones very simply, with a little dry brush work indicating their green weather-staining. The shadows on the grass were a mixture of Payne's grey and raw sienna and they helped to pull the foreground together.

5 Choosing and Developing Subjects

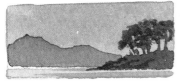

Beginners can make life difficult for themselves by choosing unsuitable subject matter. They are naturally attracted and impressed by magnificent views and grand panoramas but because they lack experience, they do not always appreciate the demands such subjects can make. They try to include everything in the complex scene before them, only to find their painting quickly becomes overworked and laboured. There is no reason why they should not choose impressive landscapes as their subject matter, but if they do, they should realise that the key to success lies in simplifying and concentrating on the broad effect rather than recording detail. Watercolour is the ideal medium for capturing the atmospheric tones and colours of the landscape, but its beauty and freshness are all too easily lost through labouring after unnecessary detail. It is often better to select a small part of a spectacular view than attempt to capture the entire panorama.

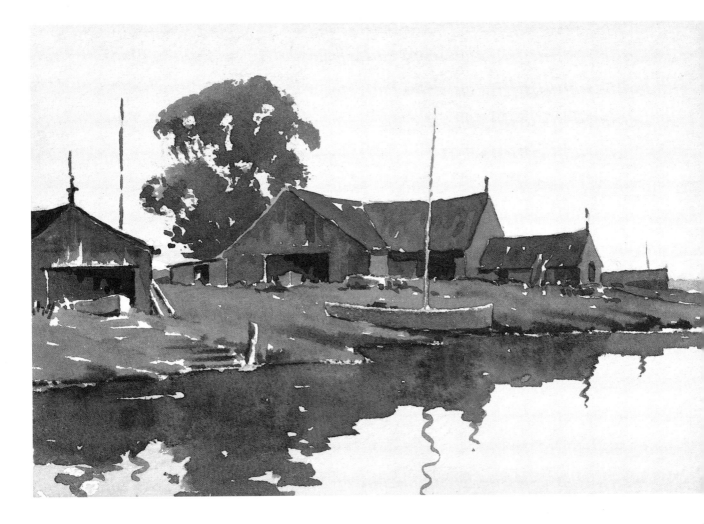

CHOOSING SUBJECTS

Students who experience difficulty in finding suitable subject matter for painting sometimes ask me how I go about choosing subjects for my own work. It is not an easy question to answer. To some extent, if you can cultivate an enquiring mind, subjects choose themselves, and in time experience will tell you the type of subject that lends itself to watercolour treatment. It is a mistake to set out on a painting trip with too settled an idea of what you hope to paint, for that ideal subject can be frustratingly elusive. Far better to train yourself to be receptive and sensitive to artistic stimuli of all kinds, for if you succeed in doing this, you will never be short of subjects to paint.

The best advice I can give on the question of choosing subjects is to paint what appeals to *you*. Do not be put off by the knowledge that a particular subject has been painted many times before by other artists and may be regarded by some as hackneyed. It will only be an artistic cliché if your treatment is too conventional and uninspired, not if you have something fresh and personal to say about it. At the same time, you will probably do better to find something more

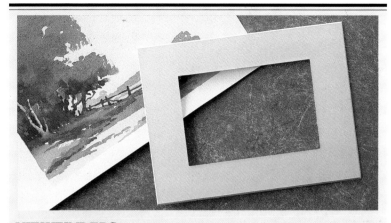

VIEWFINDERS

A simple viewfinder can be an invaluable aid to separating promising compositions from their complex settings. The type of viewfinder I have in mind is simply a piece of card – perhaps an offcut of mounting board – with an aperture about the size and shape of a postcard cut from the centre. When held up against a broad panorama, it helps you to isolate likely subjects by blotting out their surroundings. You can vary the extent of the view within the frame by simply moving the viewfinder towards or away from your eye, and the resulting variation in scale relative to the frame will help you discover a pleasing composition.

The usefulness of this simple device is not confined to panoramic landscapes – it can be equally helpful in locating likely sections of more modest scenes. If you have not yet used a viewfinder I would urge you to give it a try.

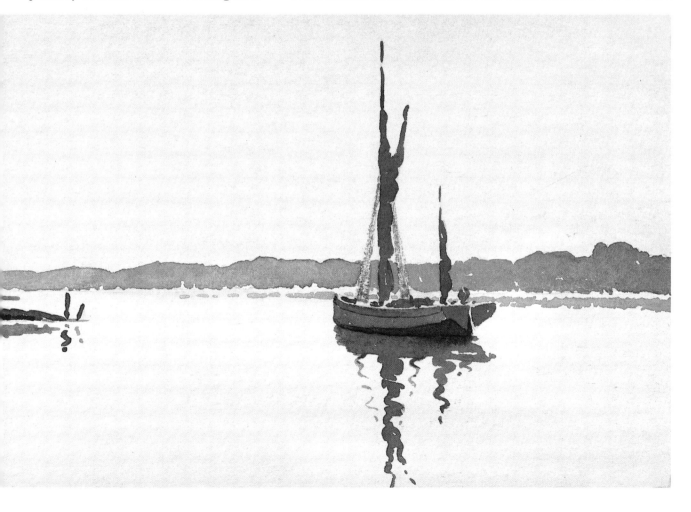

original for yourself. Do not confine your search to 'picturesque' subjects which you know will prove popular (and, perhaps, saleable) but look for interesting compositions which may well be formed by everyday objects.

I was recently giving a criticism to the members of an old established art club and it soon became evident that there had been a club outing to a local well-wooded beauty spot. There were a number of paintings of excellent standard of this woodland scene and it was interesting to see how many of the members had placed a small figure, dressed in red, against the predominantly green background – no ignorance of complementary colour theory there! The majority of the paintings were perhaps a little predictable, with a woodland path leading the eye into the heart of the leafy landscape, flanked by carefully placed trees on either side. I could not escape the feeling that the artists had been so impatient to get down to their painting that insufficient time or thought had been given to the search for more interesting and impactive compositions.

The painting that caught my eye was a glimpse of a sun-dappled glade, viewed through the tracery of a nearby bush and the bold verticals of a few saplings in the foreground. The arrangement of the passages of sunlight and shadow produced strong tonal contrasts which reinforced the lively and original composition, and although the painting was perfectly representational I was struck by its strongly developed pattern before becoming aware of its subject matter. The artist, as I expected, had a strong feeling for design and this was equally apparent in the other paintings he showed me.

Such original and highly individual treatment of a familiar scene is usually the result of thorough observation and a determination to get the feel of the subject. If, on the other hand, the observation is cursory and superficial, the resulting painting will in all probability be tame, uninspired and rather obvious – however skilful the painting technique. When an artist has studied his subject profoundly and made an effort to look beneath the surface, his painting will have far greater depth. It will reveal something of what he felt and this can invest the most ordinary subject with magic.

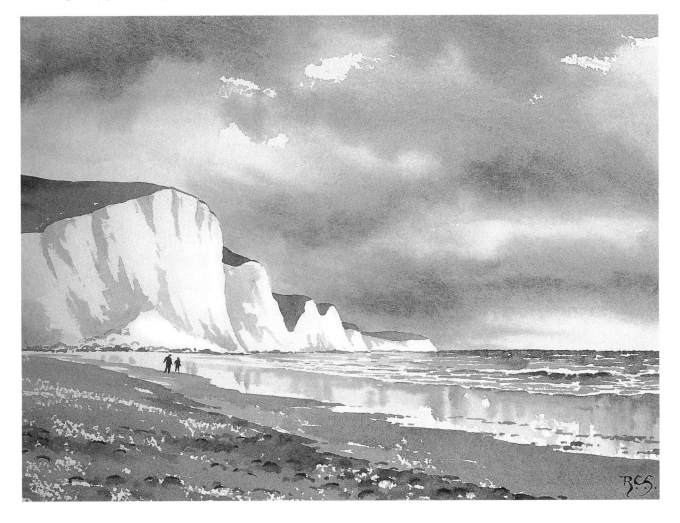

Painting is not simply a matter of reproducing accurately what we see before us – the camera can do that much more quickly and efficiently than we can. It is rather the attempt to capture the very essence of a scene through light, colour and composition. Whatever it is that moves us to paint a particular subject in the first place must be preserved at all costs and no painstakingly added detail must be allowed to obscure it. If we aim for spontaneity and simplicity and make up our minds to omit irrelevant detail, our original idea is much more likely to shine through and convey to others something of our personal reaction to our subject.

This personal reaction to a subject can be profound and we should take advantage of it. It sometimes happens that we come across a scene that cries out to be painted but, despite all our good resolutions, we have not even a sketchbook with us. Even the briefest sketch on the back of an envelope is better than an opportunity irretrievably lost, and we should do everything we can to get

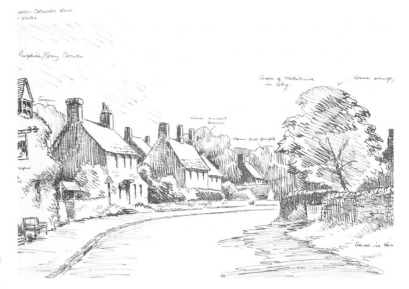

something down on paper. The sketch of the Cotswold village street (above) was made at breakneck speed with a borrowed fountain pen, but, with the scribbled colour notes, it enabled me to produce a satisfactory watercolour.

COTSWOLD VILLAGE STREET

THE SEVEN SISTERS
The white cliffs of Kent and Sussex have inspired many painters and it is not hard to see why this should be so. In this painting I adopted a very low viewpoint in order to emphasise the height and grandeur of this impressive natural formation. I also opted for a dark sky, to contrast with the shining white of the chalk. The expanse of glistening sand is a foil for the adjoining stretch of darker, drier sand and also accommodates the brilliant reflections of the white cliffs, against which the two tiny figures stand out boldly to provide scale.

Apart from its pale, grey shadows, the chalk is just untouched paper. The sea is very simply treated, with the white of the watercolour paper representing the lines of breakers. A broken wash, with a few random pebbles added, suggests the rough texture of the foreground shingle.

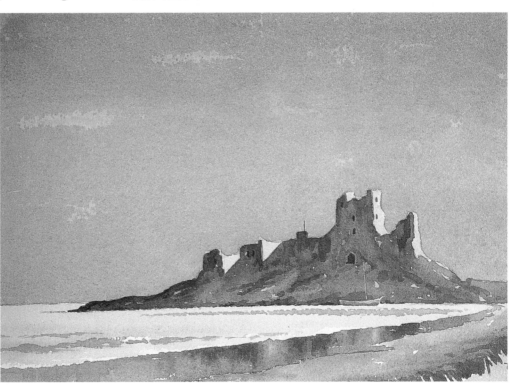

BAMBURGH CASTLE
A low evening sun was just catching the ramparts of this splendid old castle when this view was painted. The sky behind was several tones deeper than the pale sea and the dramatic scene made a perfect subject for bold and decisive
treatment. The sky was ultramarine and light red, with the proportion of the warmer colour increasing towards the horizon, and I applied a variegated wash, taking care to leave chips of white to denote the shining stonework of the castle. I soon realised the
sky needed to be darker than I had made it, so once it was dry I applied a second wash, this time leaving a few wispy clouds. The sunlit stonework was just pale raw sienna, while the shadowed areas were various deep combinations of
ultramarine, light red and burnt sienna. The strip of wet sand reflected the deep tones of the castle and the lighter grey of the sky, and provided foreground interest.

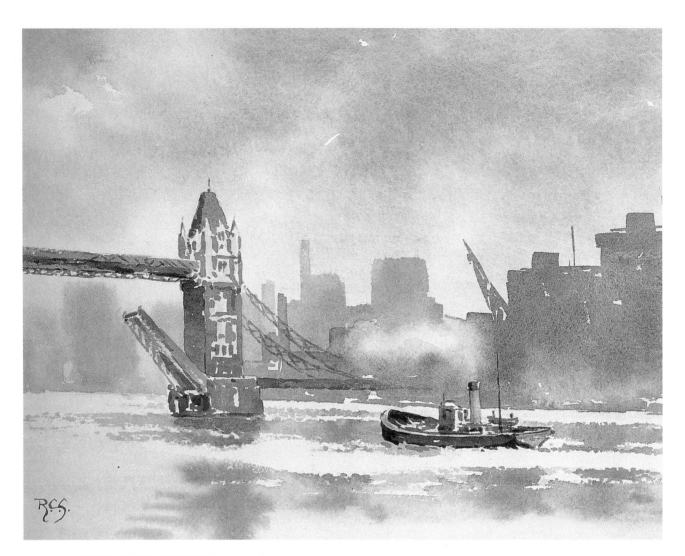

DEVELOPING SUBJECTS

Once I have decided upon my subject and spent some time studying it in depth, my approach is to make several quick sketches from different vantage points, as already described. It usually happens that one of these will produce a more interesting composition than the others and I concentrate on this, adding tone, eliminating superfluous detail and, if necessary, varying the positions of some of the elements to produce better balance. Some painters have a deep-seated antipathy to altering subject matter in this way, but I have no such inhibitions. Unless there is some special reason for preserving accuracy, the demands of a harmonious composition are paramount, and if this means moving a tree or a building, so be it.

Rough, preliminary sketches not only enable you to work out your composition, they also assist you in planning your tonal balance and in exploring your subject in depth. How much of this information you then transfer to your watercolour paper is another matter. In the early stages, fairly detailed drawing will give you confidence, but, as we have already noted, the less drawing there is, the greater the chances of expressive brushwork giving your painting character and panache. A lot will depend upon the type of subject. Groups of buildings, bridges, boats and so on call for a certain amount of fairly accurate draughtsmanship if perspective and compositional errors are to be avoided. Simple landscapes comprising fields, hedges and trees are another matter and just a few lines, noting the position of the horizon and the main elements, are all that are required.

The rough pencil drawings opposite are typical examples from my own sketchbook. You may find it helpful to make some sketches yourself of scenes from your neighbourhood, featuring a street corner, a stretch of river, a farm, a pastoral scene and anything else that takes your fancy. Tackle each subject from several different vantage points and decide which yields the most pleasing composition. As your experience increases, you will rely less on careful drawing and more on expressive brushwork.

THE POOL OF LONDON

Misty landscapes have a particular fascination for the watercolourist and I resolved to keep this one as simple and direct as possible. I quickly painted the sky in pale, pearly colours and carried the wash down to the far bank of the river. I then began putting in the shapes of the distant buildings, using ultramarine, light red and burnt sienna in varying proportions. The sky was still damp at this stage, so the shapes were soft edged and misty to the left, but became more definite and deeper in tone as the background wash began to dry out. I fed in some clear water just above the tug to represent smoke.

The river itself was even more loosely suggested and when this was dry I painted in the bridge and the boat in deeper tones, but very loosely, to accord with the rest of the painting.

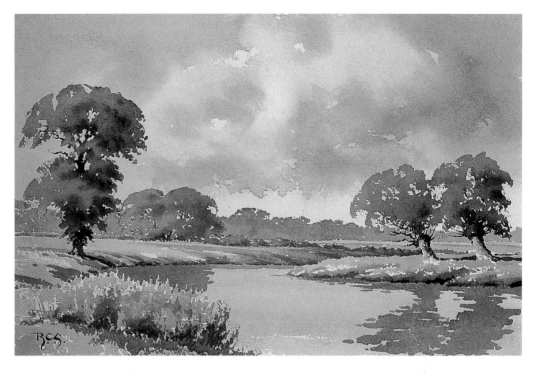

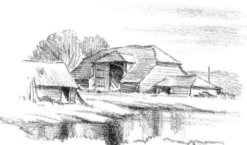

BEND IN THE RIVER

Peaceful river scenes usually lend themselves well to the technique of watercolour, for its fresh, transparent washes are ideal for describing smooth, limpid water. This painting was made on the spot one fine day in autumn. I was attracted by the diversity of colours – the russet of the trees on the left, the grey-green of the pollarded willows, the blue-grey of the line of distant trees and the greenish colour of the smooth reflections. I worked quickly with the objective of capturing atmosphere rather than detail.

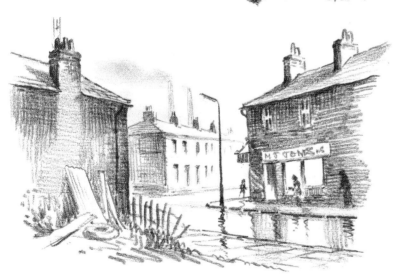

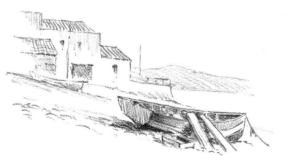

EXERCISES TO TRY

It is all too easy to concentrate exclusively on a type of subject that has a particular personal appeal. Here are a few suggestions that may encourage you to widen your horizons:

1 Seek out the type of urban subject that would not normally appeal to you, and make a sketch of it.

2 Make a quick watercolour study of the same subject.

3 Make a second watercolour study of the subject at dusk, with lights beginning to appear.

4 Use a viewfinder to isolate promising compositions in your neighbourhood and make sketches of those you like best.

KENTISH FARMYARD

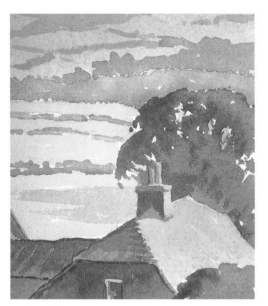

This group of farm buildings, near the Wealden village of Leeds, nestles beneath a steep escarpment which affords a splendid vantage point from which to obtain an interesting and unusual view of the subject. This type of viewpoint calls for particular attention to perspective and I drew the outlines of the buildings with some care. The positions of the trees and clumps of foliage were indicated but their forms were very roughly sketched, as I planned to capture their broken outlines with the brush.

This high-level view has another advantage; by enabling the painter to look down on the roofs and fields, it helps him to see them as constituents of a strongly defined and satisfying pattern. The geometric shapes formed by the roofs, the spaces between them and the patchwork of fields beyond combine to produce this interesting design.

Palette
raw sienna
light red
ultramarine
Payne's grey
burnt sienna

STAGE 1

A viewpoint from which one can look down upon the subject presupposes a high horizon and here it is little more than a quarter of the way down the paper. Notice how the depth of the fields decreases with distance – the effect of perspective. If you tackle a subject such as this and wish to check the perspective of the buildings by the method described in Chapter 3, remember that it is the true *horizon you need and not the apparent horizon. In this painting, the true horizon is considerably below the outline of the distant downs.*

Because the sky occupies a comparatively small area, its treatment must be restrained.

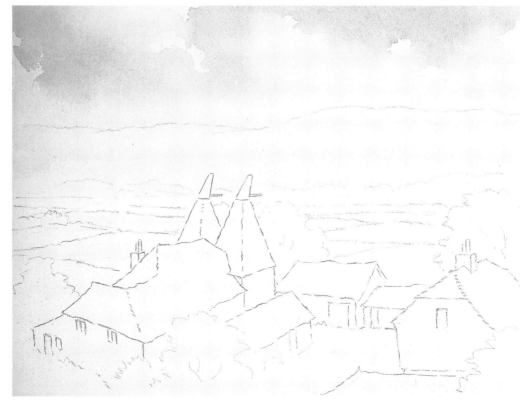

STAGE 2

My next step in the painting was to establish the distant downs and this I did with a pale wash of ultramarine and light red, with raw sienna replacing the light red towards the bottom, where the local colour of the grass was just apparent. I brought this wash down to the strip of warm-coloured woodland, and when it was dry, added, quickly and directly, some indication of distant woods and lines of hedge with a slightly stronger version of the first wash.

I put in the dark forms of the trees before tackling the patchwork of fields. Even though these fields were much lighter in tone than the trees, some evidence of the underlying wash would still have been visible if I had painted over them. Nor did I want to leave gaps for the trees, as I find this inhibiting and much prefer to establish tree forms with free brushwork that does not have to be fitted into such spaces. The trees were varying mixtures of Payne's grey and raw and burnt sienna. When they were dry, I put in the fields with a variety of pale washes to suggest pasture, cereal and plough-land. The hedges and the strip of woodland beyond were added quickly and freely.

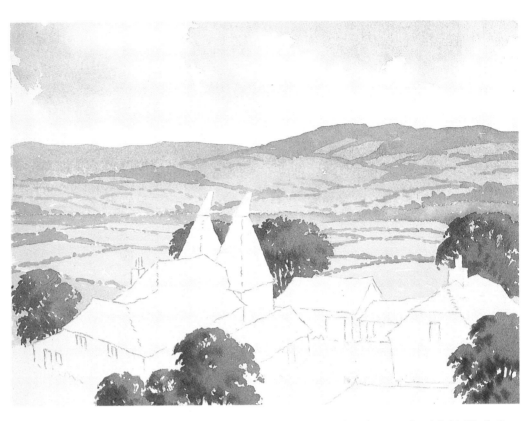

STAGE 3

The colours of the weathered brick and tile of the farm buildings, the product of Wealden clays, were rich and warm and contrasted effectively with the blue-grey of the distance to reinforce the feeling of recession. Three of the roofs were of slate and these provided another useful colour contrast. The lateral shadows were important to the composition and I took care to establish them early on. The flat washes used for the various elevations of the farm buildings looked too flat on drying, so I added texture to most of them, taking care to ensure that my brushwork followed the sloping lines of the roofs and the vertical lines of the walls.

6 All About Washes

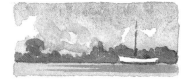

The technique of watercolour painting is based firmly upon the application of washes of various types and it is therefore essential that we know exactly what washes are and how to apply them. A wash is simply a pool of water into which a colour, or a combination of colours, has been mixed. They can be weak or strong, according to the amount of pigment they contain, and can be large or small, depending upon the area of paper to be covered. The important point to note is that all watercolour painting should be simply the application of washes of various kinds and never the application of the brush straight from the pan. There are three basic types of wash: the flat, the graded and the variegated. In practice they may be used separately or in conjunction.

TRANSLUCENCE

I have mentioned before, and it is such a fundamental point that it is worth repeating, that the beauty of watercolour stems from the white of the paper shining through transparent washes. We must therefore do all we can to preserve this lovely translucence and avoid anything that would sully it. Even dark washes may be luminous, provided they have been prepared correctly and applied boldly. So let us eschew the application of dry paint with small brushes and the dull and muddy results which follow, and determine to get the best out of our medium by the use of full washes of fresh colour.

As we have seen, several colours may be combined in one wash to produce the blend we want, but avoid including too many colours, or muddiness will begin to creep in. For this reason it is usually false economy to use residues left on the mixing palette even if they appear to be of the right colour, particularly if the wash we are preparing is destined for a luminous passage such as the sky or a sheet of water. Much better to start with fresh colour which you can be confident will provide a really translucent wash.

Another enemy of freshness and luminosity is the use of water that has become dirty and it is surprising how some painters continue using water that has begun to look more like soup. This can sometimes happen in the field if an insufficient supply has been taken, but there is no excuse for it

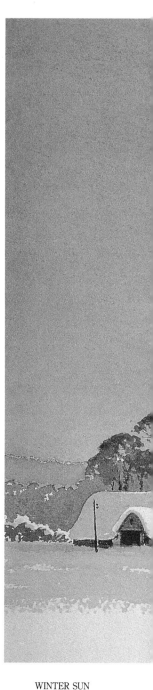

WINTER SUN
Although the sky in this painting appears a warm, pinkish grey, the temperature was very low and the painting was done from memory in the comfort of the studio. My first step was to cut out a circle of masking tape and apply it to the paper where I wanted the sun to be (I could equally well have used masking fluid for this purpose). I prepared two sky washes, one of light red with just a touch of raw sienna, the other of ultramarine and light

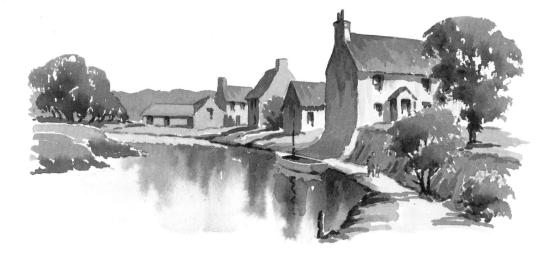

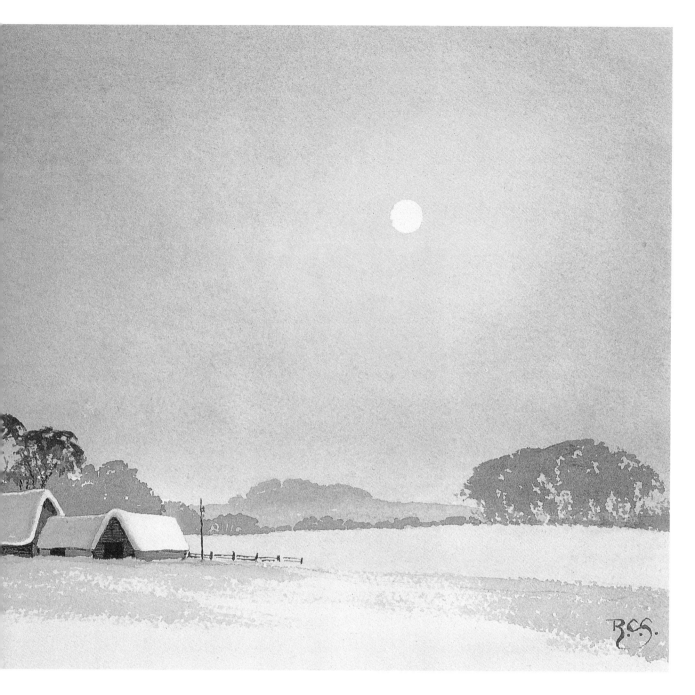

red. I started applying the first, in concentric circles round the masking tape, and when I had reached a point about 2in (5cm) from my 'sun', I began dipping my brush in the second wash. In this way I obtained a soft transition from the warmer to the cooler, deeper colour. When this sky wash was dry, I removed the masking tape to reveal a circle of white paper, which made quite a convincing sun.

in the studio. I make a practice of having two jars of water, one for mixing with paint and the other for washing brushes.

A point to remember is that watercolour fades appreciably on drying and washes that look just right in the liquid state can easily dry out to look weak and unconvincing. Allowing for this factor becomes second nature with experience, but if you are in any doubt, first try out your wash on an offcut of the same paper as you are using. This is much more satisfactory than applying a second wash to a weak initial wash, for in watercolour some freshness is lost with each subsequent application of paint. This is not to say that washes cannot be laid one over another to achieve particular effects, but as a

general principle it is better to say what you have to say in one wash rather than two or more.

One of the reasons why beginners are inclined to use rather dry colour in their watercolour work is that they feel it is easier to control. Another is that they are keen to get on with their painting and liquid washes do take much longer to dry. This is a problem, particularly when painting in a humid atmosphere. In the studio, an electric hair-drier can speed up the drying process and no harm will result, unless the nozzle is held so close to the paper that the excessive heat dulls the paint. In the field the only remedy for a slow-drying wash on a humid day is patience!

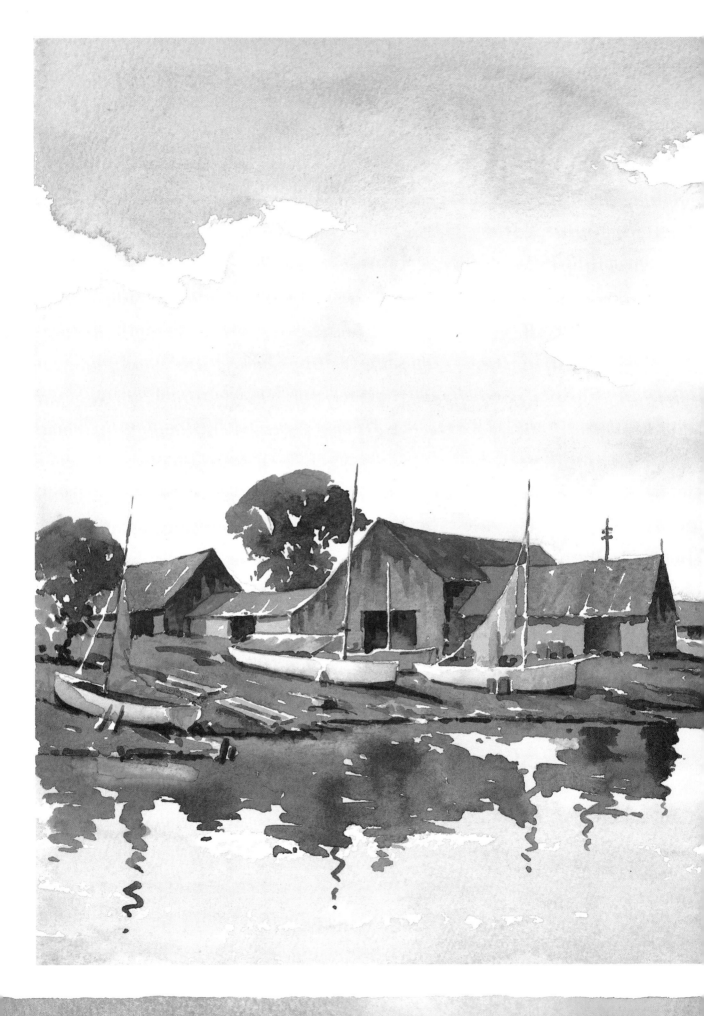

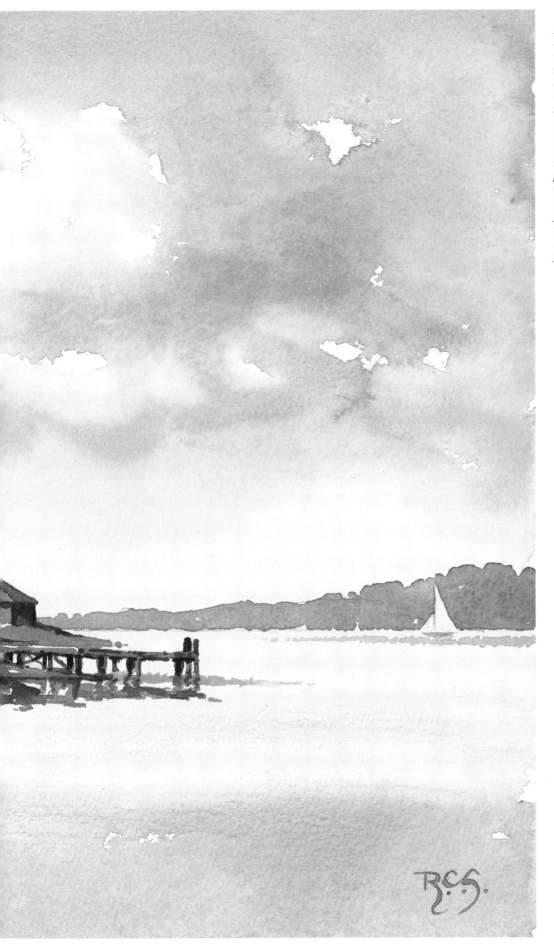

ESSEX BOATYARD
*Much of this painting
consists of a pale,
variegated wash – a
mixture of ultramarine
and Payne's grey at the
top, through raw sienna
at the horizon and back
to pale blue at the base –
though some cloud has
been introduced to
interrupt the smooth
gradation of colour. The
nearer elements and
their reflections were
painted in strong tones
in order to register
effectively against the
pale background wash.*

Once again I used masking tape, but this time I applied a strip right across the paper, to protect the horizon. The sky was basically a variegated wash, from dilute raw sienna at the top to ultramarine and light red above the horizon. While it was still wet I painted in the clouds on the right with a slightly cooler version of the second wash, and left it all to dry. With the same wash, I then painted in some more definite cloud shapes, softening some edges with clear water, but allowing others to remain hard.

I repeated the variegated wash procedure for the calm sea, but used marginally cooler versions of the original washes. When they were dry, I applied horizontal strokes of a large brush charged with the second wash to indicate cloud shadows in the distance and smooth wave forms in the foreground.

The sailing barge and its reflection were added in deeper tones against an area of radiance and are balanced by the heavy clouds on the right.

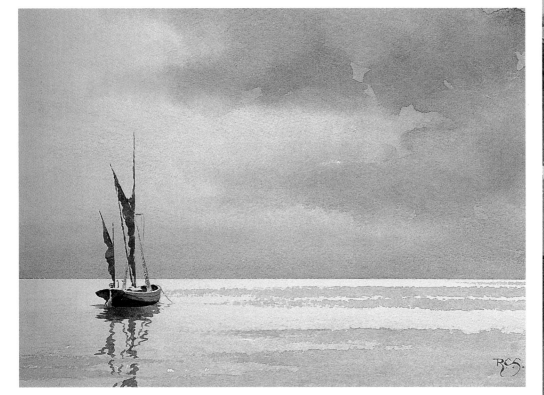

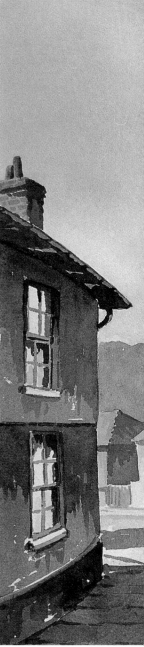

THE FLAT WASH

A flat wash is one in which the colour is laid down evenly and uniformly.

To prepare a simple flat wash, first judge the amount you require and then pour that amount of water into a saucer or into one of the depressions in a mixing palette. It is best to overestimate the amount required rather than the reverse, for nothing is worse than running out before your wash is complete; a hastily mixed addition is unlikely to match the first exactly and the incomplete wash will in any case have started to dry. Add the pigment, a little at a time, until you are satisfied with the tone. Avoid applying too much paint to begin with or you may have to add a lot more water and end up with far more of the wash than you require, resulting in waste. This is all too easily done with some of the stronger, staining colours. Mix

THE CATHEDRAL OF THE MARSHES
For this sky I prepared two washes, one of very dilute raw sienna, the other of Payne's grey, and applied them with two large brushes, allowing them to merge together softly, but carefully avoiding the church tower. When they were dry, I applied a second wash of Payne's grey around the tower, softening it into the original wash with clear water in places, but leaving just a few hard

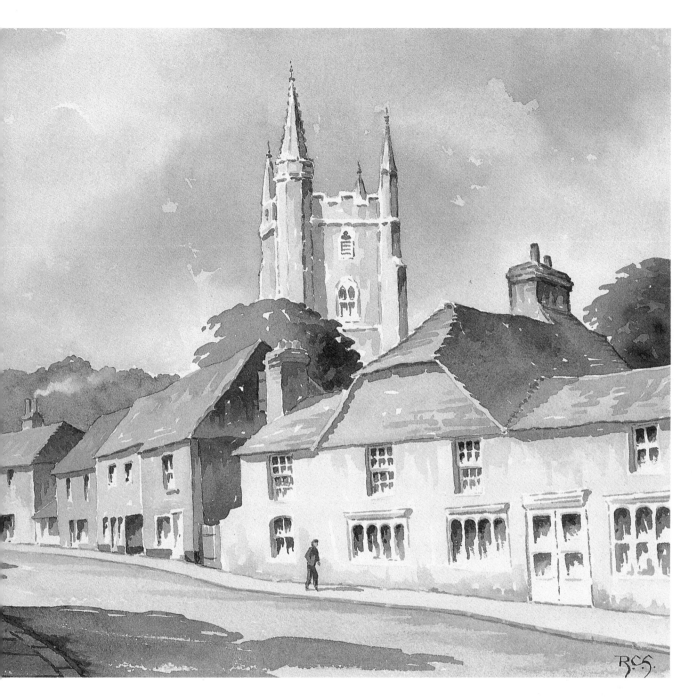

edges for the sake of variety. The resulting deeper tone made the tower stand out boldly, even after I had painted it in pale washes of raw sienna, light red and a touch of ultramarine.

The sunlit houses below were painted in pale tones, with stronger washes of much richer colour for the shadowed sides. Notice the reflected light in the windows of the house on the left of the painting.

the paint and the water together thoroughly to ensure no traces of paint remain undissolved, for these can ruin the clarity of your wash.

Before beginning to apply the wash, it is important to decide upon the angle at which the drawing board should be held. If the angle is too steep, the wash will simply stream down the paper; if it is too level, there will be insufficient gravity for it to flow at all. Artists differ widely in this respect, but I find an angle of about 15 degrees from the horizontal is about right.

Using a large brush, perhaps a 1in (2.5cm) flat, start applying the wash in a horizontal band at the top of the paper. A bead of paint will collect at the lower edge of

this brushstroke – the effect of gravity – but this will be taken up by the following stroke of the recharged brush. Continue in this way down the paper.

I normally start each brushstroke at the opposite side of the paper to the last, to ensure an even distribution of paint, since more paint is laid down at the beginning of the stroke than at the end. If I am laying down a wash for a sky, I may well want one side to be paler than the other, to suggest the direction of the sun, and in this case all my brushstrokes will start at the side I wish to be slightly darker.

Moistening your paper before starting to paint will overcome any possibility of unevenness occurring.

THE GRADED WASH

The next type of wash used in watercolour painting is the graded wash. This is simply a wash in which the tone varies evenly from dark to light, or vice versa. A graded wash is useful for tackling skies, where the effect of the atmosphere is to decrease the tone as the horizon is approached. The procedure is similar to that of applying a flat wash, but here a little clean water is added and mixed into the wash for each succeeding brushstroke. If working from light to dark, the reverse applies and more pigment is progressively added to the original pale wash. In the example below, the Payne's grey becomes paler toward the horizon.

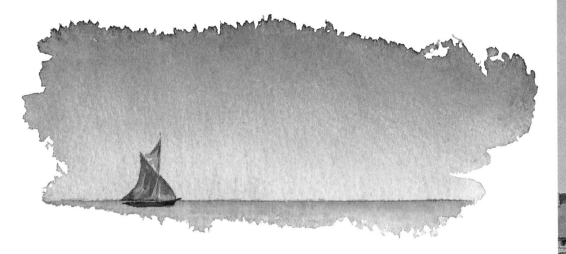

THE VARIEGATED WASH

The third type of wash is the variegated variety. This is similar to the graded wash, but instead of gradually changing to a paler (or deeper) tone, it merges evenly into a different colour. To achieve this effect, washes of the two desired colours are prepared in advance and the brush charged with the first. With each successive brushstroke, less of the first wash and more of the second is taken up until, at the bottom, little of the first colour remains.

With practice you will master the wash technique and you may wish to begin by trying your hand at the three washes I have demonstrated. With some rather absorbent papers, it is not easy to get a smooth gradation of tone or colour and there may be some stripiness. One way of getting over this difficulty is to dampen the surface of the paper evenly before applying paint.

Mastery of these basic washes is fundamental to successful watercolour painting. They may, of course, be modified in all manner of ways; for example, by adding further colour, wet in wet. This is where the fascination of the medium really begins. We shall be considering this and other exciting watercolour techniques in later chapters.

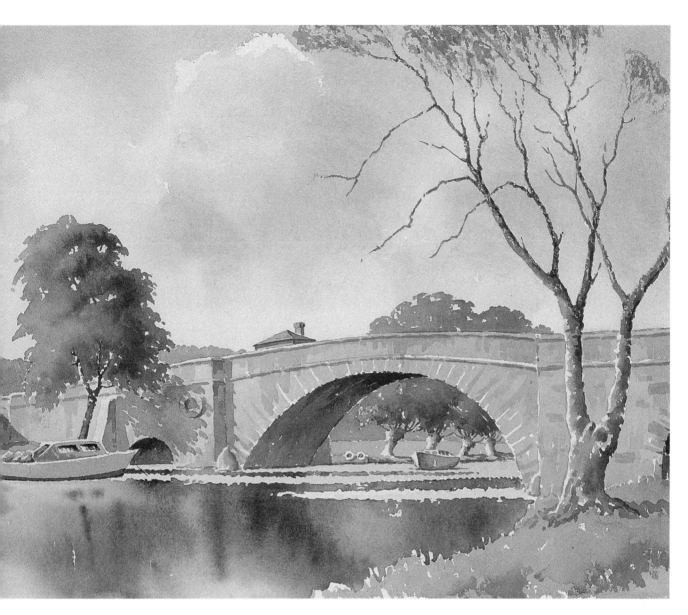

THE HALFPENNY BRIDGE

This painting of the old toll bridge at Lechlade was a commission for a visiting American who fell in love with the peaceful upper reaches of the Thames. To create an atmosphere of tranquillity I opted for an understated sky with gentle cloud shadows, and a smooth expanse of water with soft reflections. The pale colours of the sky were allowed to blend and only in two places are there any hard edges to the clouds. With the exception of the light-toned bands of wind-ruffled water below the bridge, the river was established in one variegated wash containing the colours of the objects above. These colours were applied quickly so that they merged together softly. I then added a few darker accents while the wash was still wet, to provide form.

EXERCISES TO TRY

Skill at handling washes is basic to good watercolour practice. The exercises that follow should help to develop your skill:

1 Lay down a full, flat wash of ultramarine.

2 Try a graded wash, using the same colour, but adding water as you quickly work down the paper.

3 Now apply a variegated wash, starting with ultramarine and ending with raw sienna. Did these first three washes look fresh and even on drying, or did patchiness and unevenness creep in? Continue practising until you become fluent!

4 Add a quick impression of trees and hills in deep tones to your last wash, which should then convincingly suggest a clear sky.

THE GRAND CANAL

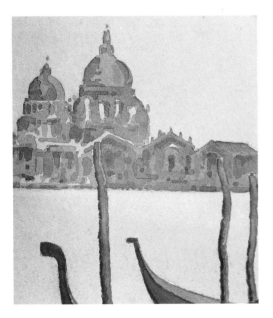

This much-painted view of Venice, copied from an old sketch, gave me the opportunity of applying a warm, variegated wash over the whole paper, with a few local variations. The strong evening light becomes increasingly dim towards the left of the painting and here the deeper tone helps to balance the main weight of the composition, which is on the right. The largely horizontal format is helped by the strong vertical form of the mooring poles, particularly that of the left-hand pole. This mooring pole, with its reflection below and the dome and cupola immediately above, ties the composition together.

Palette
raw sienna
light red
ultramarine
burnt sienna
Winsor blue

STAGE 1

I prepared three generous washes for the sky and water. The palest was raw sienna with a little light red. The intermediate contained rather more light red and just a touch of ultramarine while in the third wash, the deepest in tone, the proportions of light red and ultramarine were both increased. I started applying the palest wash on the right and moved across the paper to the left, gradually increasing the proportions of the second wash, then the third as I worked.

While the paper was still wet I introduced a little of the deepest wash to the foreground water and put in a soft, horizontal shadow on the left. I then lifted out a little colour, with a moist brush, just below the buildings on the right

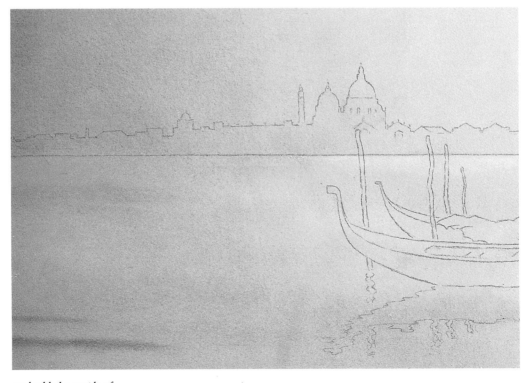

and added a couple of ripples, wet in wet, in the left foreground. I then allowed everything to dry.

The far shore contained a mass of buildings and although I wished to indicate their presence, I did not want to get involved in a lot of meticulous detail. I therefore decided to adopt a 'shorthand' approach which merely suggests form and leaves much to the imagination. For this purpose I prepared three washes of ultramarine and light red, the palest being the warmest and the deepest being the coldest. I applied the pale wash first, starting on the right, but as I worked my way towards the left, I increased the proportion of blue in the wash, so that the cooler colour would suggest recession. With the second wash I picked out a few intermediate tones and increased the proportion of light red in the centre of the painting for the sake of variety. I finally added a little of the deepest wash to indicate door and window openings and to give a little more prominence to the domes of the Santa Maria della Salute.

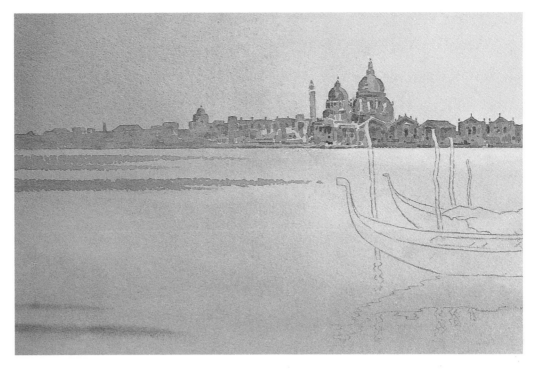

STAGE 3

All that remained now was to paint the foreground gondolas, the mooring poles and their reflections, using deep, warm colours to bring them forward and provide contrast with the soft greys of the far shore. The browns were various combinations of burnt sienna, light red and ultramarine, and the dark accents were stronger mixes of the same colours with a higher proportion of the blue. The warm green of the tarpaulin was a deep wash of Winsor blue with raw and burnt sienna. The reflections were a similar colour, with rather more blue. In conditions such as these, reflections often take their colour from the water itself – a muddy green – rather than from the objects being reflected.

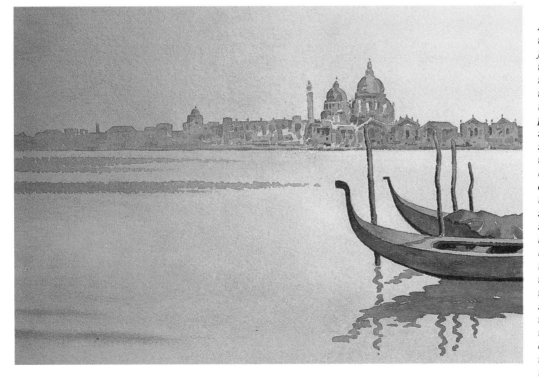

7 More Watercolour Techniques

In the last chapter we considered the basic washes of watercolour. We shall now turn our attention to the ways in which they may be employed in the painting process and how their treatment may be varied to obtain particular effects. Later in the chapter we shall examine further watercolour techniques such as broken washes and dry brush work.

We have already noted how the quality of the light influences the colours of the landscape and how vital it is to ensure that the two are in harmony. The warm colours of a late summer evening cast a glow over the countryside, enhancing the rich hues of old brick and tile, russet foliage and ripe corn. One way of ensuring that all parts of the painting are in colour harmony is by carrying the warm colour of the sky down over the whole paper. This basic wash will impart a warmth to washes laid over it and the fragments which receive no further colour will help to unify the painting. A development of this technique is to vary the overall wash to take account of the local colour in different parts of the painting. At this stage, we will only be concerned with the paler tones of these local colours, the deeper tones required for shadows and so on being applied later. This treatment really consists of a more complex version of the variegated wash.

To begin with, we need to analyse the paler local colours in all parts of the scene – sky, fields, trees, buildings, water, lanes and

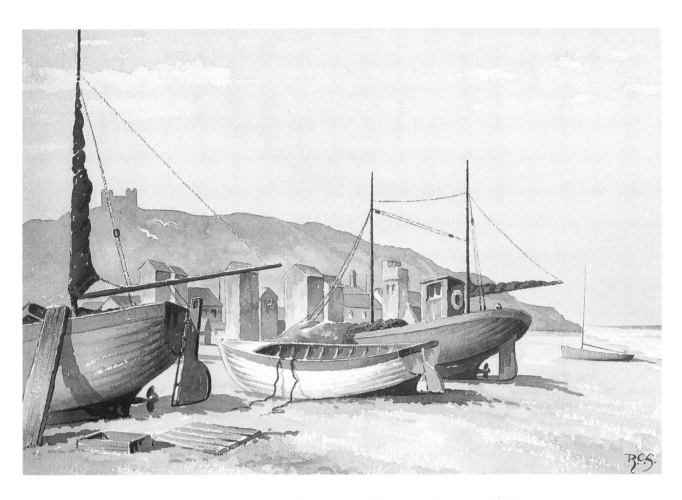

anything else in the landscape. We then prepare suitable washes for each of these local colours, remembering that we are only interested at this stage in broad areas and are not concerned with detail of any kind. We then apply these washes, quickly and boldly, over the whole paper, letting the colours merge softly where they meet. This is the point at which delightfully soft effects may be obtained by dropping in deeper colours to suggest the misty forms of distant hills, trees and so on. This technique, known as wet in wet, is described more fully in the next chapter.

When the variegated wash is dry, we may lay further washes over it, working all the time from light to dark. In the watercolour medium, washes should always be liquid and should be laid quickly and with the lightest of touches. It is always good practice to lay washes in this way, with a minimum of modification; this applies with even greater force when working over an area that has already been painted. If the under-wash is disturbed by too much fussy brushwork, the result is bound to be muddy and unsatisfactory.

A further advantage of applying a variegated wash to the whole of the paper is that we are no longer faced with areas of white paper, which can be distracting. This broad approach is likely to result in a degree of inaccuracy and some of the local colours may not end up precisely where they should be. Do not worry! This has to be accepted as part and parcel of the technique and it would be a mistake to attempt any alteration – the increased accuracy would not compensate for the loss of freshness and spontaneity. If the painting method is kept free and loose, and any temptation to tightness resisted, little harm will be done.

EXPLORING WASHES

When we were considering washes of various types in the previous chapter, we noted that they could be modified to produce varying effects and we shall now explore these techniques. Let us start with a variegated wash, with ultramarine at the top blending gradually into raw sienna at the bottom. This could well represent a clear sky. If we now wish to introduce some soft-edged clouds, the appropriate colours – perhaps a mixture of ultramarine and light red – could be dropped into the still-wet wash. This is perhaps not quite as easy as it sounds, for success depends very much on correct timing. If we attempt to add the clouds while the variegated wash is still too

THE NET SHEDS OF OLD HASTINGS
An underwash of raw sienna was carried down over the whole painting, with the exception of a few areas such as the sea and the white boat where I wanted the colour to remain cool. When this was dry I applied a second wash to the sky, ultramarine with a little light red at the top softly merging into raw sienna and light red above the horizon, with a few ragged shapes left unpainted to represent fleecy clouds. Broken washes of various combinations of raw and burnt sienna, light red and ultramarine served for the rough texture of the foreground shingle.

A variegated sky wash with grey cloud superimposed, wet in wet.

wet, the grey will spread into the wash and be virtually lost. If, on the other hand, we leave it too long, and the background wash is beginning to dry, there will almost certainly be a thoroughly unsatisfactory mix of hard and soft edges to our cloud.

The effects that this technique *can* produce when properly handled are so useful in watercolour painting that conscientious practice to explore and master the technique is worth while. The above illustration is an example of a sky painted in this manner. If some of the grey is lifted while still wet by pressing gently with a dry brush or a tissue, and replaced with a wash of palest raw sienna, the effect of sunlit clouds may be produced, as below.

Another problem we have to contend with is the effect known as 'flowering', or sometimes 'cauliflowering'. This happens when we apply too liquid a wash to a background that is just beginning to dry. Here, the water in the second wash is carried by capillary action into the drying wash, taking pigment with it. When it reaches a still drier area of the first wash and can travel no further, the pigment is deposited in unsightly concentrations. To prevent this unwanted state of affairs occurring, we must ensure the second wash is less liquid than the first. It is all a question of judgement, and judgement only comes with practice and experience.

The way in which these washes behave will depend not only on the skill of the artist and his sense of timing but also upon the temperature and degree of humidity of the atmosphere. These are variables which we cannot control, but due allowance has to be made for them. In very dry conditions, for example, more water has to be mixed with the washes to compensate for the shorter drying time. Papers and paints react in different ways and this is a good reason for sticking to watercolour papers and a limited palette of colours with which we are familiar.

MASKING FLUID

Full washes have to be applied quickly and boldly, and this makes it difficult to paint round small shapes we may wish to preserve, for example white gulls against a stormy, grey sky. Unless we resort to using body colour, such as Chinese white, the only practical alternative is masking fluid. This is a liquid latex which we can paint over such small areas and then safely apply our broad wash over the top. When everything is dry,

Another variegated sky wash but with cloud showing sunlit areas.

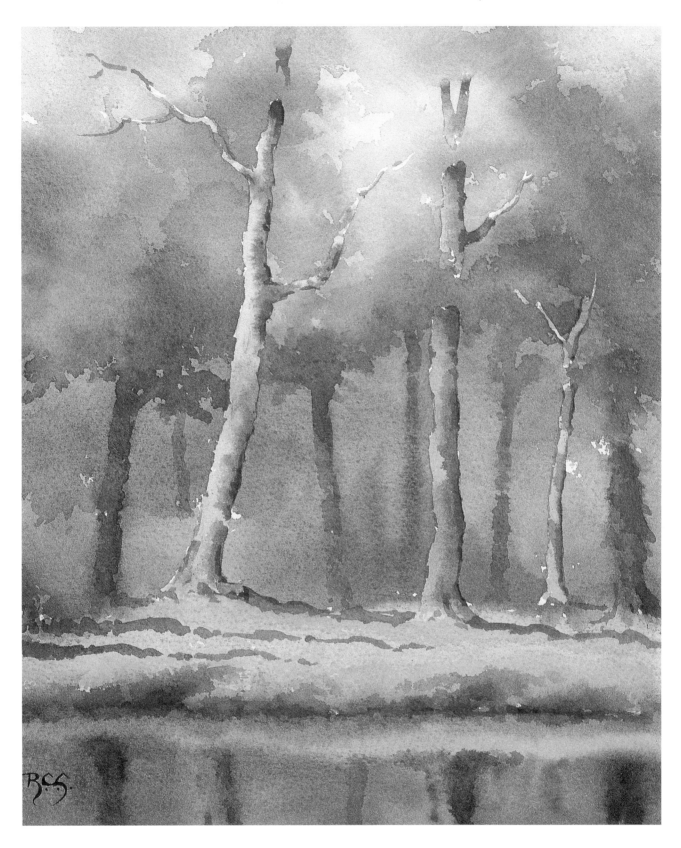

WOODLAND POOL

Once again a wash of pale raw sienna was carried down over the whole paper and allowed to dry. Masking fluid was then applied with an old brush to the three foreground tree trunks so that they might stand out crisply against the misty effect I planned for the background. I used a variegated wash for the background foliage, with various combinations of raw sienna, Winsor blue, ultramarine and light red, with more raw sienna for the sunlit foreground grass. When the paper was beginning to dry I painted in the dim tree shapes, using Payne's grey for the shadowy foliage and deep ultramarine and light red for the trunks, obtaining the desired variety of hard and soft edges. When everything was completely dry, I rubbed off the masking fluid with my forefinger and then applied a little colour and shading to the tree trunks which it had protected.

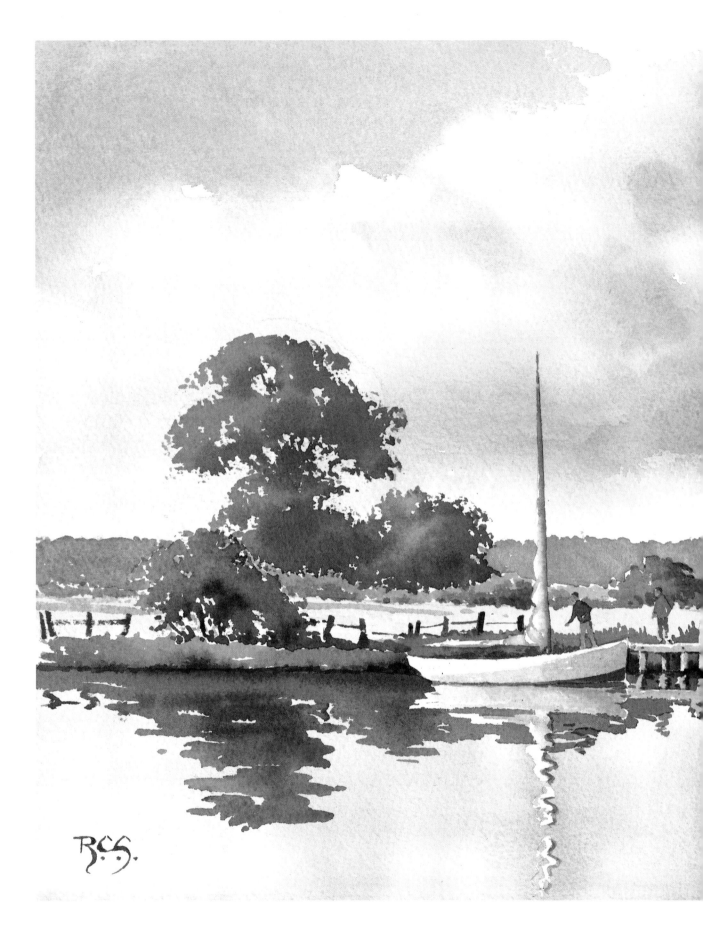

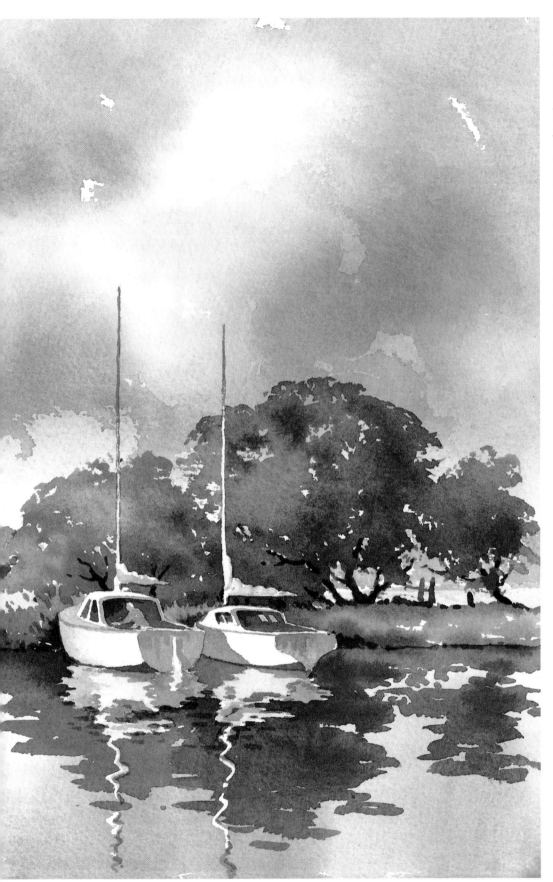

My aim in this painting was to contrast the pale tones of the boats with their background of dark foliage and to capture something of the limpid feel of the water. The boats required fairly careful drawing and I preserved the shapes of the masts and furled sails with masking fluid.

I used two washes for the water. The first established the soft reflection of the sky in pale tones. When this was dry, a stronger, hard-edged wash indicated the nearer reflections, with indented edges to suggest the rippling surface of the river.

MORE WATERCOLOUR TECHNIQUES 87

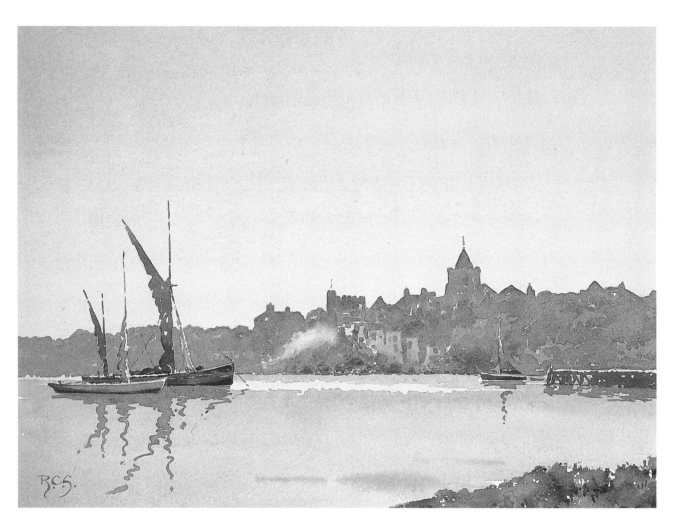

we can remove the latex by gently rubbing with the forefinger, to reveal areas of white untouched paper.

Some words of warning here: masking fluid should not be used on the softer watercolour papers, which tend to lose surface fibres when the dried latex is removed. Also, however quickly the fluid is removed from brushes after use, some deterioration is inevitable, so only cheap or part-worn brushes should be used for this purpose.

THE BROKEN WASH

As their name suggests, broken washes are less continuous and complete than flat washes. They are produced when the brush is less fully charged and is dragged rapidly over the surface of the paper, leaving ragged edges, gaps and chains of white dots where the paper remains untouched. Naturally this effect is most easily obtained by using paper with a rough surface.

Broken washes, an example of which is shown below, can be extremely useful in suggesting textured surfaces. Portraying foreground detail is a perennial trap for the inexperienced, who all too easily become embroiled in painting individual pebbles, seed heads, blades of grass and so on. Skilful handling of broken washes and dry brush work will enable you to achieve bold and telling effects quickly and with little apparent effort. In watercolour, spontaneous techniques score every time over the more laboured approach.

EVENING LIGHT, RYE
In this study of golden evening light, I applied a wash of raw sienna, slightly warmed with light red, over the whole of the paper, adding just a little Payne's grey towards the top. Small areas of this warm yellow appear in various parts of the composition, such as the narrow band of pale water, the tops of the boats and the landing stage, helping to give the painting unity.

A broken wash for bold treatment of foreground.

A grey rock, produced by an initial flat wash with added dry brush work.

Broken wash and dry brush treatment of tree and bush forms.

DRY BRUSH WORK

With dry brush work, the brush is less fully charged than for a broken wash, and is again drawn quickly across the paper, engaging the little bumps in its surface but missing the little depressions. The dry brush effect is used to suggest texture and it is a useful method of giving character to a surface which appears too bland. Despite the expression 'dry brush work', the brush should not be so dry that the marks it makes are dull and muddy. A fuller brush *is* more difficult to control, but held flat to the paper and handled with speed and dexterity, the effects it produces can be both textured and lively. Above, an impression of a rock is shown before and after the application of some dry brush work. The second illustration demonstrates how the technique can indicate the forms of trees and bushes.

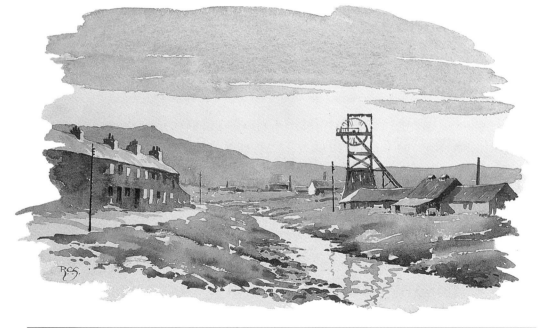

MINING VALLEY
A rather more obvious example of the overall preliminary wash, here a variegated wash was applied over the whole paper, with raw sienna at the top and an increasing proportion of light red as the wash was carried down. Quite a lot of this initial wash received no further colour, particularly in the foreground, and this helped to give the painting a feeling of cohesion and unity. Even cool washes applied over the basic wash, such as the ultramarine and light red of the distant shoulder of hill, have a warmth which relates them to the rest of the painting.

EXERCISES TO TRY

1 Lay down a variegated wash to represent a clear sky – perhaps Payne's grey merging into raw sienna – and while it is still wet, drop in some grey to represent soft-edged clouds.

2 Apply prepared washes of palest raw sienna for sunlit clouds, of ultramarine and light red for cloud shadows, and of ultramarine for blue sky and allow them to merge here and there.

3 Try a broken wash of raw and burnt sienna below one of these skies, to suggest stubble.

4 Add texturing to your stubble with some dry brush work, using burnt sienna with a touch of Payne's grey.

FARM BUILDINGS AT HEAVERHAM

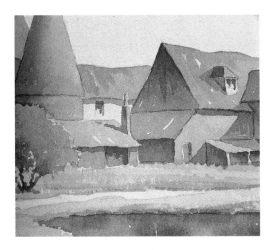

When there is a particularly strong colour in the light, for example, when a golden evening glow suffuses the landscape, it sometimes helps to carry the colour of the sky down over the whole of the paper. This helps to unify the painting and ensures that the dominant sky colour influences every part of the scene below.

In this group of farm buildings, reflected in the farm pond, this is what I have done. The overall warm yellow wash will, of course, influence the colours laid over it and any chips of the original wash left uncovered will help it all to 'hang together'.

Palette

raw sienna
light red
ultramarine
Payne's grey
burnt sienna
Winsor blue

STAGE 1

I placed the group of buildings a little left of centre and balanced them with a deep-toned oak tree to the right. The sky will be reflected in the pond below the gap between the farm buildings and this tree to give the water greater tonal contrast and interest. The farm track leads the eye right into the centre of the group.

I prepared a generous wash of raw sienna and light red and applied it evenly over the whole paper. While it was still moist I dropped in some warm grey (a mixture of ultramarine and light red) and this produced the soft-edged clouds. I made very sure that the grey wash was less liquid than the overall wash, to avoid any danger of 'flowering'. These soft clouds helped to relieve the rather too insistent warm yellow of the sky.

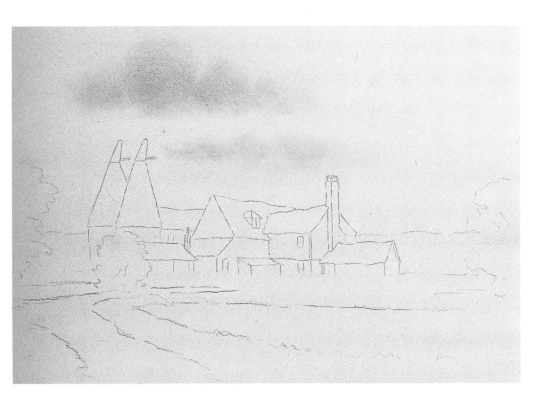

STAGE 2

My first step in this stage was to establish the two oaks and the hazel bush, again using the roughness of the paper to assist me in capturing the broken outlines of their foliage. The distant line of downs was a flat wash of ultramarine and light red.

Most of the farm buildings were old brick and tile and for these I used varying washes of burnt sienna and light red, adding a hint of green (raw sienna and Winsor blue) to suggest moss and algae to the lower courses. The warm, lateral light produced an interesting pattern of lights and darks and I determined to make the most of these to obtain a three-dimensional effect. The shadowed walls and roofs were deeper washes of light red and

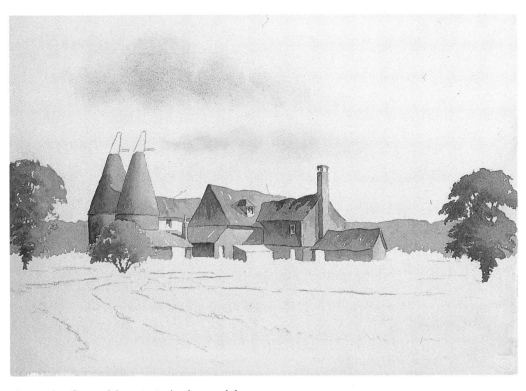

ultramarine. Some of the flat planes looked rather too flat on drying, so I introduced a little texturing here and there, taking care to follow the slope of each roof and the line of each wall.

STAGE 3

The grass was put in with quick horizontal strokes of a large brush loaded with a mixture of Winsor blue and raw sienna. This left quite a lot of the base wash untouched, particularly in the foreground, to suggest the rough surface of the grass and link different parts of the painting together. A broken wash of a slightly warmer colour was added to strengthen this textured effect and then the shadows were established with a wash of Payne's grey and raw sienna. At this stage the farm track was just the original pale wash of raw sienna and light red and all it needed was a broken horizontal wash of light grey.

I left the water until last so that I would know exactly what had to be reflected. I then prepared several washes to correspond roughly with

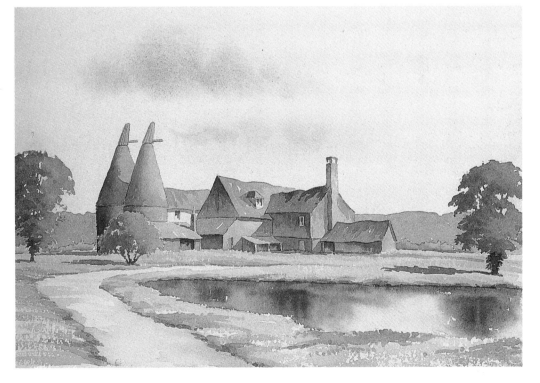

the colours of the objects above and applied them as quickly as possible, so that they all merged together. As this variegated wash was just beginning to dry, I added a few darker accents with vertical strokes of the brush.

8 Mist and Mystery

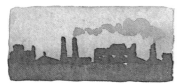

The beauty of watercolour lies in its capacity to convey the soft effects of mist and fog and the subtleties of atmosphere. Imaginatively used, it can capture the pearly hues of light percolating through broken cloud or the brilliance of the noonday sun. Some of Turner's watercolour sketches show us how, in the hands of a genius, the medium can create breathtaking images of light and colour. When we see watercolour used in this masterly way, we realise afresh the vital importance of striving to interpret light and its effect on the landscape, and the relative unimportance of recording irrelevant detail. If we keep this conviction constantly in mind, it will help us to use the medium with feeling and imagination.

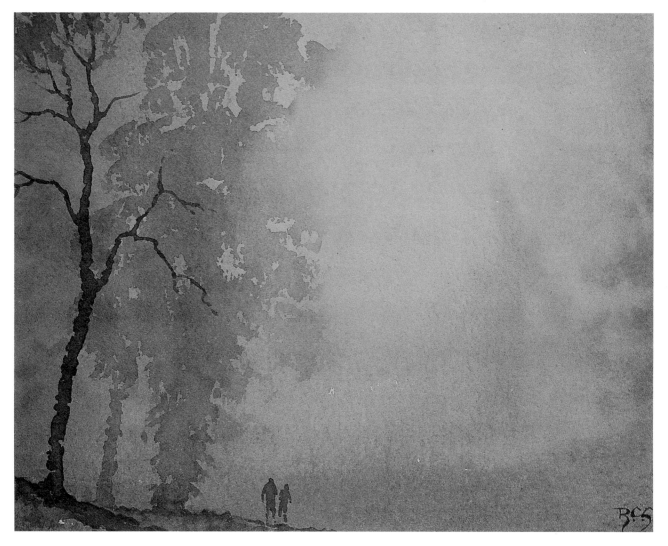

EVENING MISTS

In this painting my aim was to capture, as simply as possible, something of the atmosphere of a warm, evening sun percolating through misty woodland. A wash of palest raw sienna merging into light red touched with ultramarine served for the sky and while this was still wet a rather stronger wash of the last two colours was dropped in, to suggest the mysterious outlines of the distant trees. When the paper was dry I painted in the nearer trees in warm grey silhouette, having previously wetted the area of luminous sky to obtain a soft-edged effect and an impression of radiance. I then put in the left-hand tree in deeper tones of the same wash and the two small figures, which provide a focal point and give the painting scale.

WATERCOLOUR FOR ALL

In the previous chapter the technique known as wet in wet was noted and although its detailed treatment and examination were deferred, one simple application was in fact described – the addition of grey pigment to a still-wet variegated wash to produce an impression of soft-edged cloud. In this chapter we shall study the technique in greater detail and show how its mastery can add an entirely new dimension to watercolour painting.

EXPLORING WET IN WET

We have seen that the wet in wet method is simply the addition of a second wash to a wash that has already been applied and that, because both washes are in a liquid state, the colours and tones will merge at the margin and everything will be soft edged. We have established, too, that the second wash must be in a less liquid condition than the first or an unwelcome phenomenon known as 'flowering' will result. So far so good. The next point to note is that the more liquid the washes, the softer and more diffuse will be the merging that takes place between the two.

This variation in edge definition has important implications for atmospheric painting, for it means we can vary the mistiness of our images at will. It is also easy to see how, properly handled, the wet in wet technique can indicate recession in an extremely effective manner. The paler, softer images will be the more distant, and, as definition increases, the objects so painted will appear to come forward until the nearest will be hard edged.

If, for example, we wish to make a painting of a stretch of woodland in misty conditions, we would start with an overall wash of some suitably pearly colour, and while this was still wet – but not too wet – we would drop in some pale grey to indicate the most distant trees. This would produce a soft, ethereal image, suggesting distance. Slightly nearer trees would be painted next in rather stronger tones and, because by then further drying would have taken place, the results would be rather less misty. We would use even stronger tones for still nearer trees and would continue in this manner until the background wash was finally dry, when clearly no more wet in wet painting would be possible. The nearest trees could then be put in, hard edged, in yet deeper tones and these would contrast with the progressively softer treatment of the more distant trees to create a powerful feeling of recession. This would be reinforced by aerial perspective, the use of pale, cool colours to denote distance, and stronger warmer colours, with greater tonal contrast, for foreground features. This feeling of recession would be further strengthened, of course, by the effects of linear perspective – the ever decreasing size of the trees as they recede into the distance. The painting *Woodland Track* (*see* page 97), is an example of this sort of treatment. It was painted on the spot early one autumn morning to illustrate an article for the *Leisure Painter*.

WET IN WET WASHES: STAGES OF DRYING

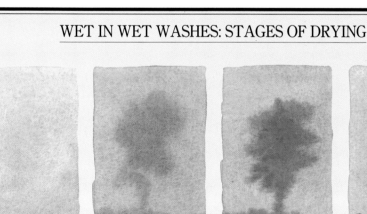

If the washes are too wet, the second wash will be swallowed up by the first and will disappear.

When only a little drying has occurred, the second wash will produce a soft and insubstantial image.

As further drying takes place, the image will become progressively more definite, though still soft edged.

Only when drying is virtually complete will the addition of a second wash result in hard edges rather than soft.

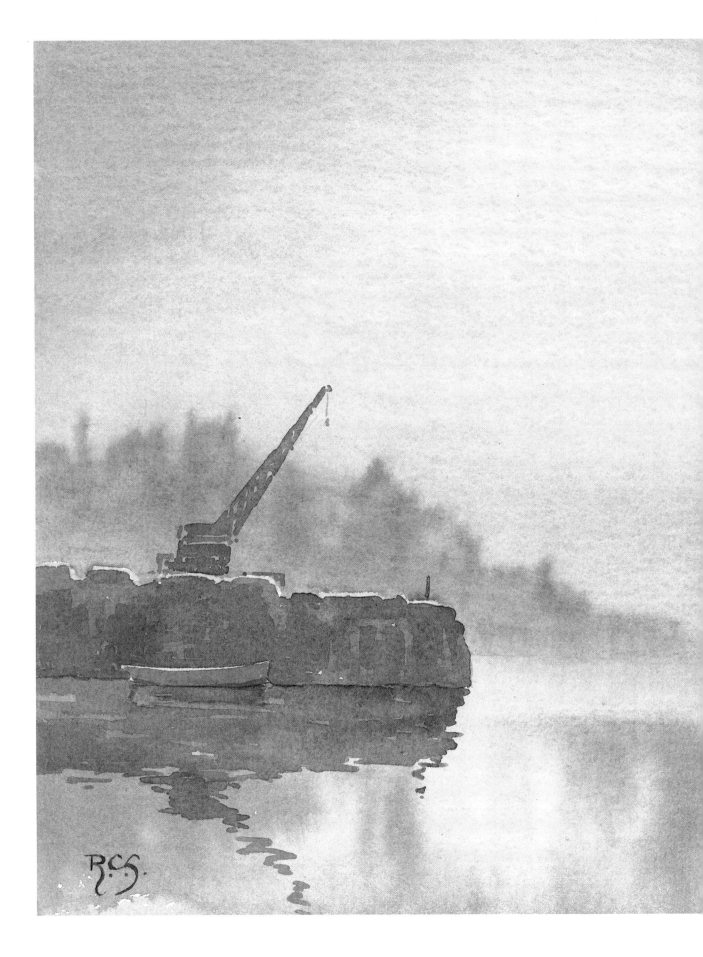

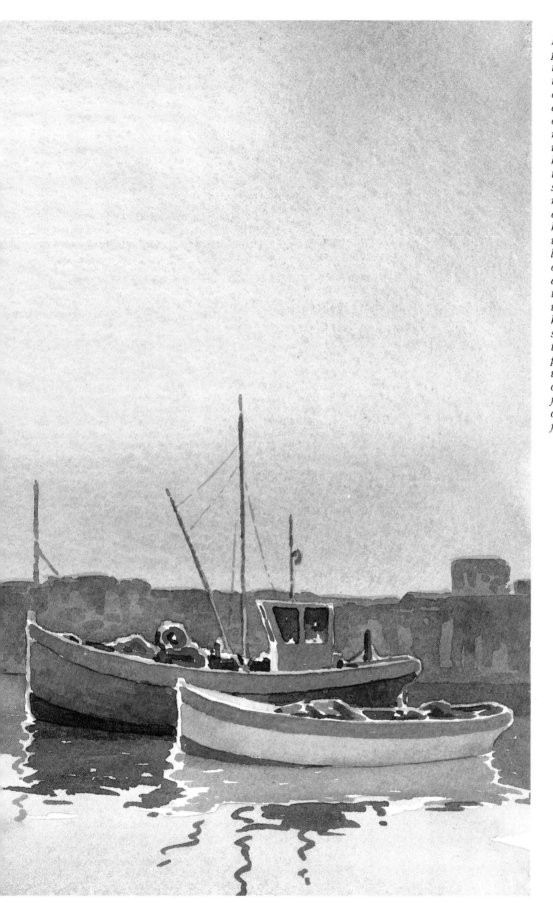

My objective in this painting was to capture the soft, pearly light and the misty outline of the distant headland. I used a pale, variegated wash of ultramarine and light red, cooler at the top, warmer just above the horizon, with an area in the centre of dilute raw sienna plus a little light red. I brought this wash down to the top of the harbour walls, where I wished to preserve the line of light along the top of the stonework. I then added deeper tones of the same grey, wet in wet, for the misty headland. The stonework, the boats and their reflections were painted more crisply, with increasing tonal contrast towards the foreground, in order to create a convincing feeling of recession.

MIST AND MYSTERY

TIMING

Timing is all important in wet in wet painting. The ability to judge the degree of dampness that will produce exactly the desired amount of merging will only come with practice and experience. If there is a lot of painting to be done before the background wash is dry, as there was in *Woodland Track*, speed of working is of the essence, and there is no time for fiddling detail. Fortunately for me, when I was painting this picture, the air was very humid, which slowed down the drying time and enabled me to put in all the soft tree outlines I wanted before drying was complete.

Speed of drying varies considerably from paper to paper. With hard-surfaced papers, which have plenty of size in their make-up, drying tends to be slow; while with softer, more absorbent papers, the surface dries more quickly. This is another good reason for sticking to a narrow range of watercolour papers, so that one gets to know their handling properties intimately. One way of judging the degree of dampness of your paper, and its readiness to accept a second wash, is to observe the precise moment when the wet shine of the initial wash just begins to dull, though it has to be said that the behaviour of different papers varies considerably in this respect.

Wet in wet painting over a broad, initial wash is not, of course, the only way to obtain soft-edged images. If, for example, you wish

WOODLAND TRACK
I painted this scene one fine autumn morning, when the sun was just beginning to break through the mist. Once again I began with a pale, variegated wash for the sky area and started to paint in the dim shapes of the trees, wet in wet. As the paper began to dry I added the nearer trees, but only when it was quite dry did I put in the foreground trees.

WILLOW
A painting in which everything is soft and misty can look rather too bland and formless. This is an example of a wet in wet painting in which some hard edges have been retained to provide contrast. A wash of pale raw sienna was applied over the whole painting down to the margin of the foreground water and allowed to dry. Clear water was then laid over this initial wash, down to the base of the trees, but some areas, particularly in the centre, were allowed to remain dry. Consequently, when the grey-green wash for the willow and the russet washes for the background trees were applied, some edges remained hard. Deeper tones were then dropped in for the shadowed areas but the dark willow trunks and branches were only added when everything was dry.

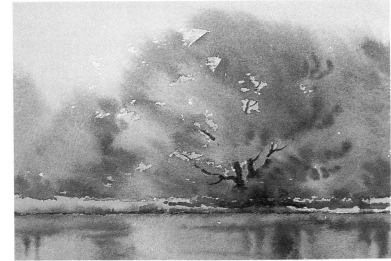

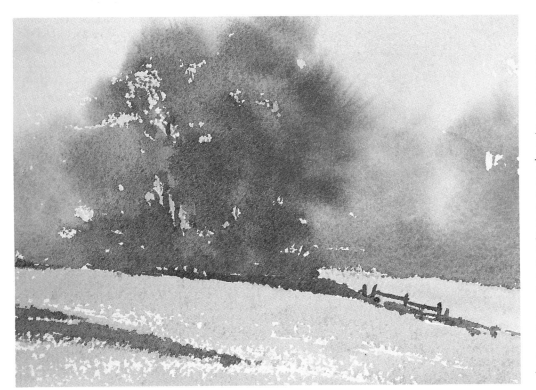

AUTUMN MEADOW
This is another example of a painting in which hard and soft edges have been combined, the technique being very similar to that described in the caption to the painting entitled Willow *(above). Here all the foliage was warm russet in colour – mainly burnt sienna – and the shadows were ultramarine and light red with some Payne's grey and raw sienna at the base of the near group. The field was a broken wash of raw sienna with a little Winsor blue added towards the top. The shadow cast by a tree off the painting to the left breaks up a rather featureless foreground.*

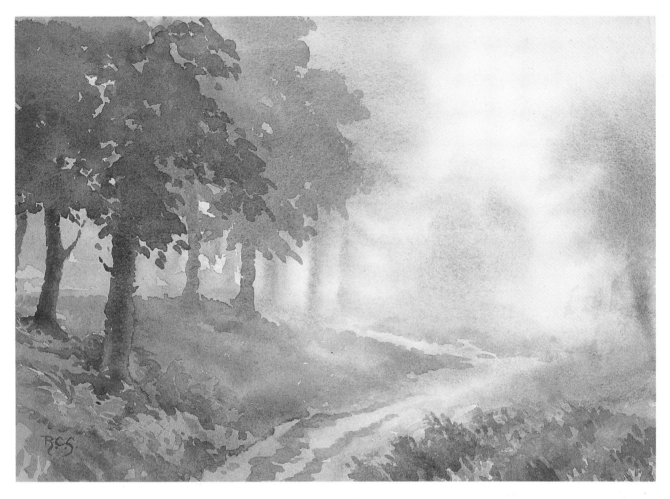

to paint a tree with a misty outline over a pale background that has already dried, it is perfectly possible to do this by damping an area rather larger than the tree you have in mind, and then applying pigment to this damp surface. Two warnings are necessary here! Firstly, a very light touch is essential if the base wash is not to be disturbed and, secondly, the greatest care has to be taken to use clean water to damp the area and to ensure that none of the applied wash finds its way to the edge of that area, or a hard ring will appear when drying is complete.

While the initial wash is still moist, colour may safely be lifted out with a damp brush – never a wet brush or the excess moisture will disturb the adjoining area and flowering will result. If a horizontal line of colour is lifted from a wash depicting a stretch of calm water, it can create the impression of a foreshortened area of water disturbed by an errant breeze.

The paintings in this chapter are examples of the way in which the wet in wet method may be used, as described in the text. Have a go at copying them or make up sketches of your own, to get practice in this all-important technique. With practice your judgement and timing will improve.

EXERCISES TO TRY

Try putting the 'wet in wet' technique into practice to produce misty effects:

1 Apply a pale wash of light red and raw sienna over most of your paper to represent an evening sky. Now paint a misty line of hills against it, perhaps using a mixture of ultramarine and light red.

2 While the sky is still moist, paint in some nearer trees in deeper tones of the same colours. They should appear more definite than the line of hills, but still soft edged.

3 When everything has dried, paint in some still nearer trees in deep, warm tones. These will be hard edged and will help the mistier passages to recede.

4 Apply a broad, horizontal wash of Payne's grey to represent a sheet of water. While this is still wet, try lifting out a horizontal line of colour with a damp brush to create the impression of a foreshortened area of wind-ruffled water.

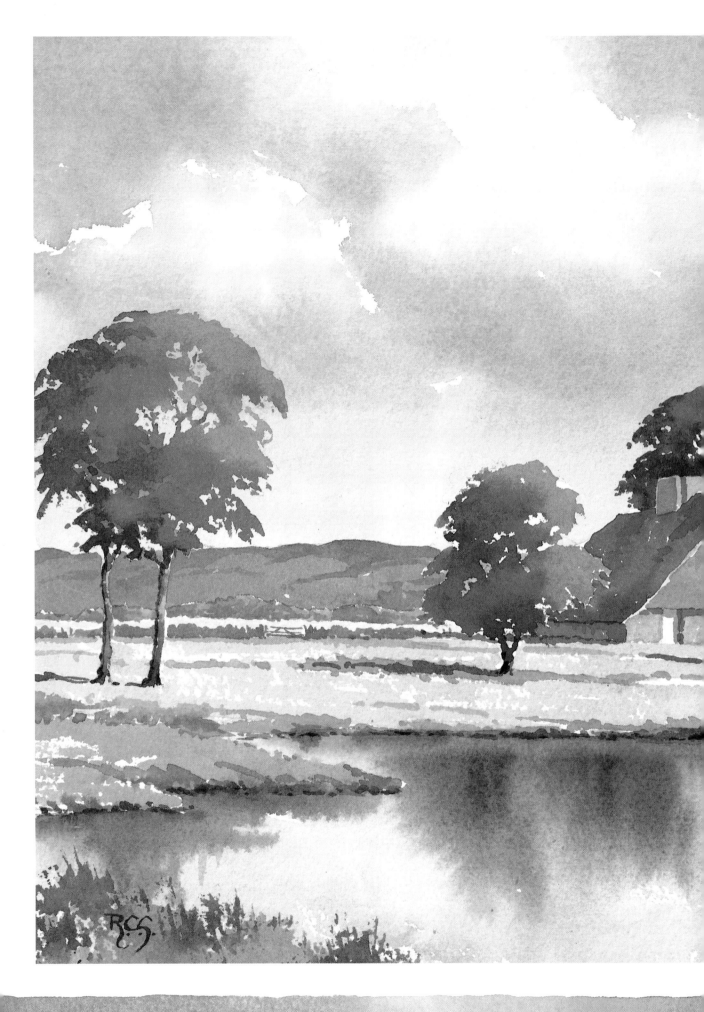

WATERCOLOUR FOR ALL

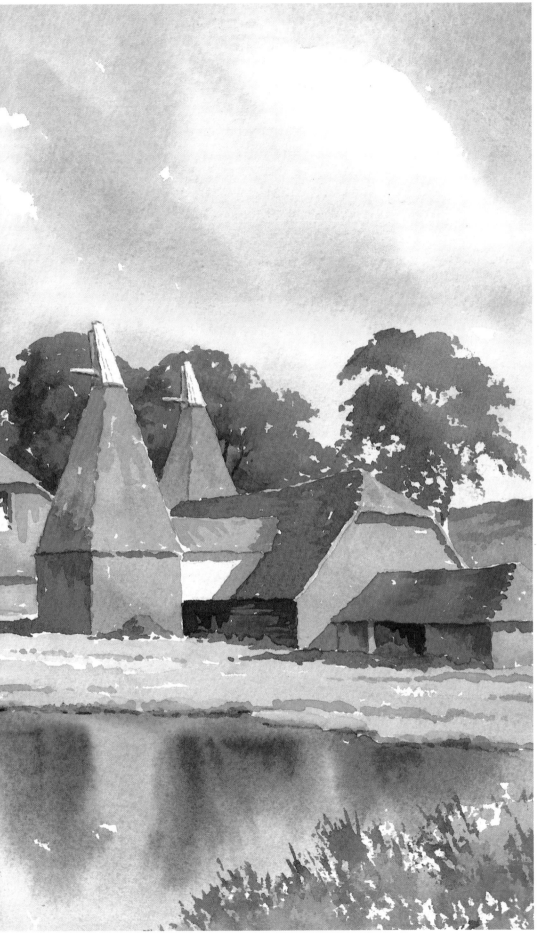

On my first visit to this delightful farm, the house, the oasts and the barns were all in full sunlight and, although the dark trees formed a useful background, there was no tonal contrast in the buildings themselves. The following morning, with the sun in the east, there was both light and shade, which made for a far more interesting group. It often pays to be patient!

TREES IN THE MIST

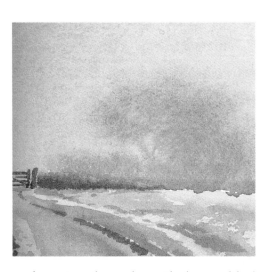

This demonstration consists of a basic exercise in the watercolour technique known as 'wet in wet' and if you have not tried your hand at it, why not have a shot at copying this simple example?

Because the technique produces a soft-edged effect, it is not wise to paint over a drawn outline. For the purpose of this demonstration, therefore, Stage 1 is simply the rough preliminary sketch on which the exercise was based, the actual painting beginning at Stage 2. Working on a wet, or moist, surface is always a chancy business, and success depends on timing and judgement; and these only come with experience. The essential point to remember is this – the *wetter* the surface, the *more* the second wash will spread, and the *drier* the surface the *less* it will spread.

Palette
raw sienna
light red
ultramarine
Payne's grey
burnt sienna

STAGE 1

This is simply the preliminary sketch. The more distant trees on the right are very soft and diffuse, and without any tonal contrast. The nearer tree on the left, although also soft edged, is more definite, with both tonal and colour contrasts. Consequently the right-hand group will be tackled first, while the initial wash is still fairly wet. Only when this wash is beginning to dry, perhaps when the shine is just beginning to go off the paper, will the nearer tree and the line of hedge below it be painted.

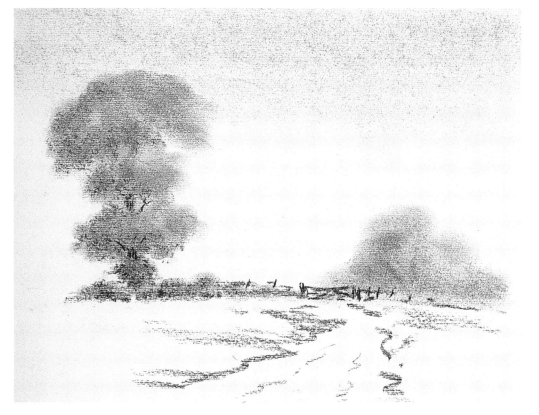

STAGE 2

The sky required a variegated wash of cool blue-grey softly merging into a warmer colour above the horizon. I prepared two generous washes, one of ultramarine with a little light red, the other of raw sienna, also with a touch of light red, and applied them in the manner described in Chapter 6. I then prepared three further washes – a pale one of ultramarine and light red for the hazy tree form on the right, one of raw and burnt sienna, and a deeper one of ultramarine and light red for the larger tree on the left.

The sky area was still very moist when I tackled the more distant tree, using a wet in wet technique, and the colour spread satisfactorily to produce an ethereal image. The drying process was under way

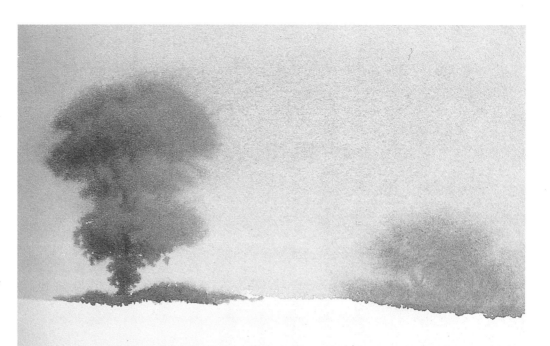

when I started applying the two washes for the nearer tree so the spread here was correspondingly less, as intended. By the time I had reached the ivy mantling round the lower trunk and the line of hedge below, the softening was minimal.

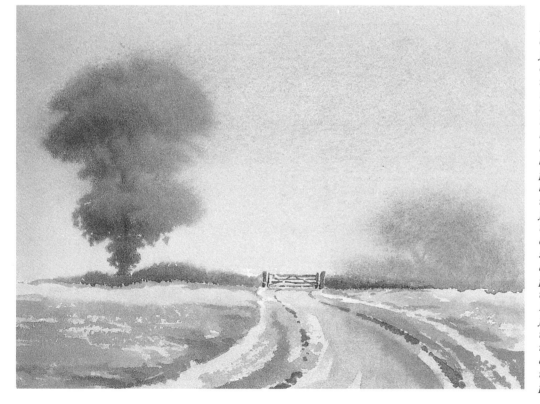

STAGE 3

It was now just a matter of painting the foreground and I decided to do this in a rather crisper manner, to provide contrast with the misty outlines of the trees. It sometimes happens that the mist hovers above ground level, softening the upper parts of trees, but leaving their bases relatively clear. The fields on either side of the track were boldly applied washes of raw sienna, to which I added a little Payne's grey in places, to produce a muted pale green. Finally I put in the winding farm track with some raw sienna and a mixture of burnt sienna and ultramarine for the ruts and the gate, which provided a focal point.

9 Painting in the Open

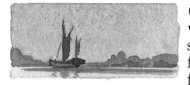

Some artists do virtually all their painting in the studio and their trips to the countryside are simply for the purpose of gathering material in the form of notes and sketches. Some isolate themselves from the outside scene by relying heavily on photographs and other illustrations for their subject matter. Others – and I am one of them – believe that direct contact with nature is more important than the comfort and convenience of the studio.

There are, of course, many days when the weather makes it impossible for the watercolourist to paint in the open and then there is no practical alternative to working indoors. Provided you have sufficient sketches with adequate colour notes and the scenes to be painted are still fresh in your mind, good work can be done in this way. Photographs can be useful for recording detail which you may not have had time to sketch on the spot, but I would not recommend using them as your sole source of information. Admittedly they can make life easier for those who find it difficult to capture the three-dimensional world on two-dimensional paper, but if you seriously wish to improve your standard, you should concentrate more on polishing up and developing your sketching skills.

Inexperienced painters do not normally produce their best work away from their source of inspiration; without their subject

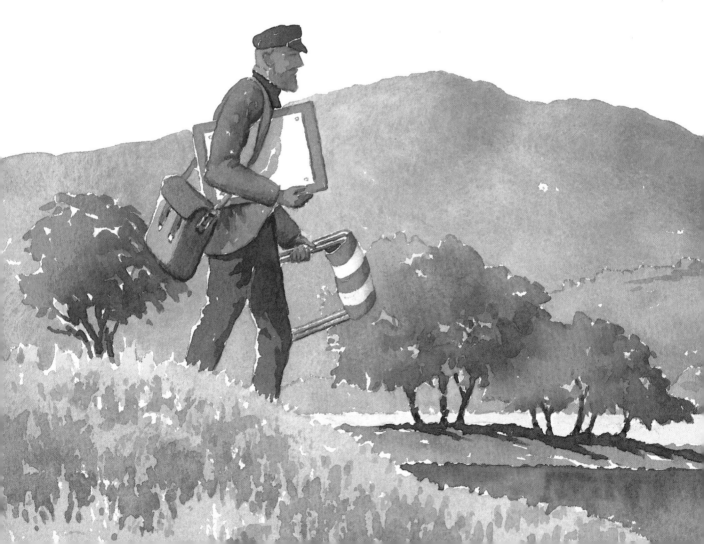

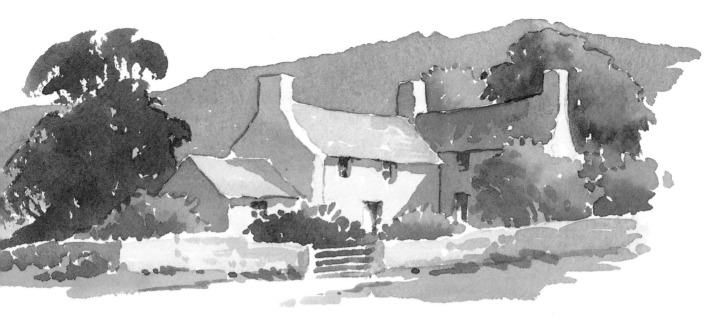

matter before them, they are inclined to play for safety in their treatment and choice of colours. Their old brick walls and tiled roofs tend to be flat washes of burnt sienna because they are not on the spot to observe the green of the moss, the yellow of the lichen and the rich colours and patina of weathering. The remedy is to paint, whenever possible, in the open, and to observe at first hand.

There is no reason why the outside scene should be the exclusive source of material and inspiration; it pays to be sensitive to visual stimuli of all kinds. Nothing should be ruled out if it sparks off a genuine artistic response. I once made a painting of a railway locomotive from a newspaper photograph. The reproduction was not a particularly good one, but the angle of the locomotive was dramatic and I felt the urge to paint it, almost in silhouette, against a patch of luminous sky, with the glow reflected in the shining curve of the foreground rails. Although the treatment was personal, the idea was sparked off by the photograph and this is a very different matter from making a laborious and precise copy of some illustration.

EQUIPMENT

Let us now assume the sun is shining and you have promised yourself a wonderful day's painting in the country. However keen you are to make a start, do make sure you take everything you need with you, at the same time resisting the temptation to take too much. A heavy load discourages reconnaissance, and searching for the right subject and the best viewpoint is an important preliminary that should not be cut short.

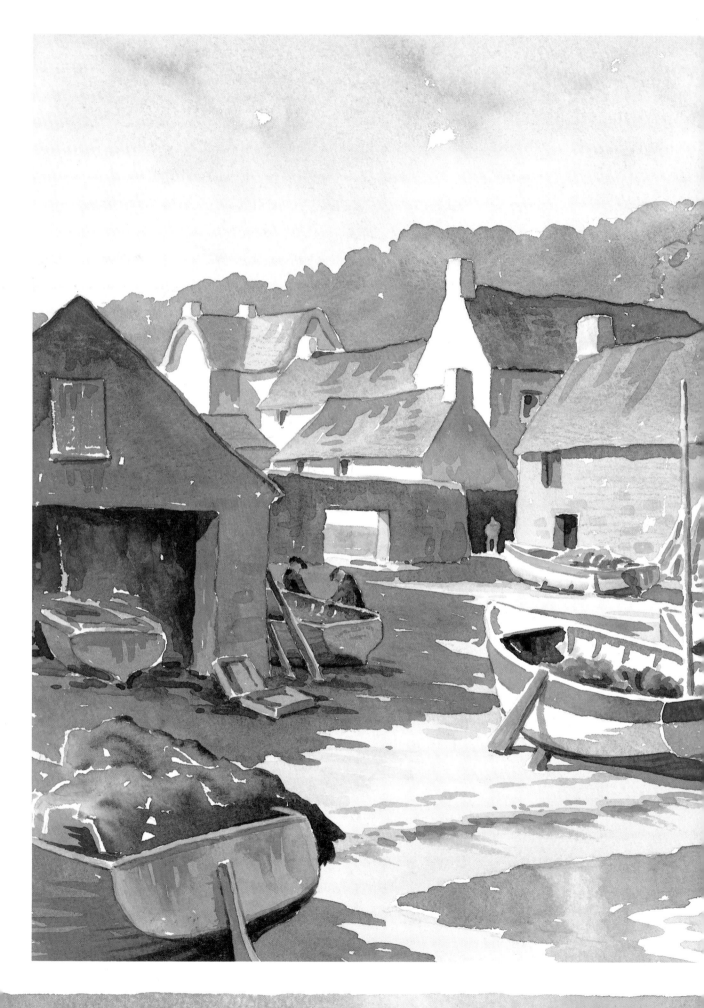

WATERCOLOUR FOR ALL

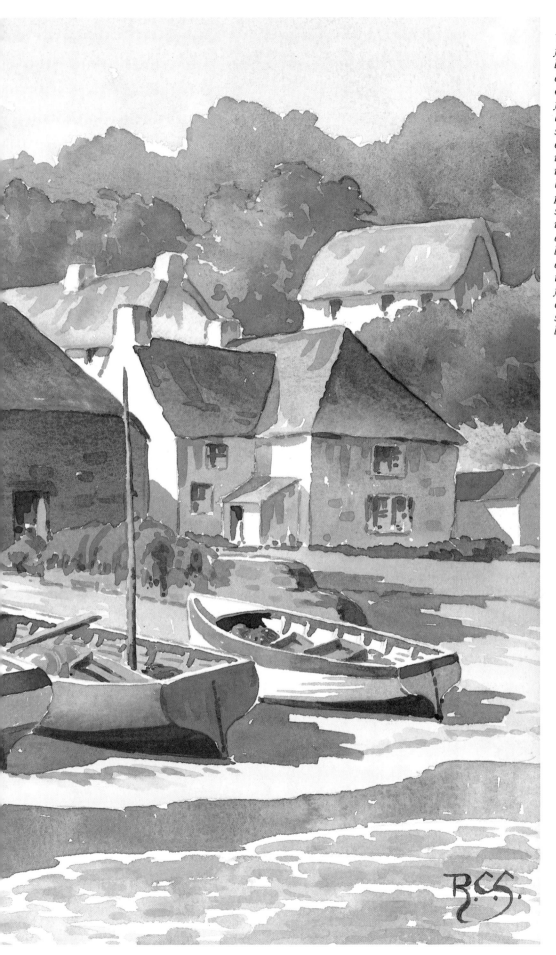

CADGWITH COVE
This painting, which first appeared as a limited edition print, is all about the atmosphere of a small Cornish fishing village, with old boats drawn up on the sand and sturdy cottages clustering round the sea inlet. The fishing boats in the foreground have been given due prominence and a few salty figures have been included to indicate some activity, albeit of the leisurely kind. Full advantage has been taken of opportunities for placing lights against darks, some of which show warm, reflected light.

I have a reasonably capacious army surplus haversack into which I can pack my paintbox, a box of tube colours, a cylindrical metal brush holder, two large jars of water (with watertight lids!), pencils, soft rubbers and paint rags. I also take a light folding stool and a drawing board with watercolour paper pinned to one side and sketching paper to the other. I do not need an easel as I always paint with my drawing board on my knee and find this helps me control the flow of liquid washes more effectively. My only concessions to personal comfort are a small bottle of insect repellent and a spare pullover.

If you prefer to work at an easel, make sure you have one of the light but sturdy

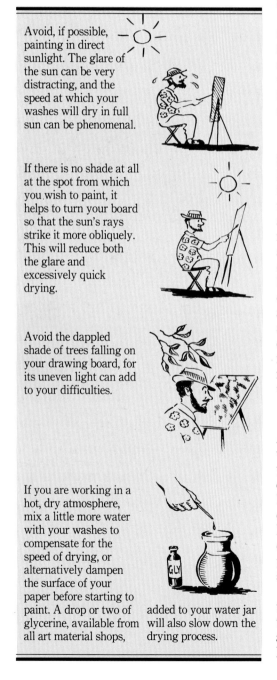

Avoid, if possible, painting in direct sunlight. The glare of the sun can be very distracting, and the speed at which your washes will dry in full sun can be phenomenal.

If there is no shade at all at the spot from which you wish to paint, it helps to turn your board so that the sun's rays strike it more obliquely. This will reduce both the glare and excessively quick drying.

Avoid the dappled shade of trees falling on your drawing board, for its uneven light can add to your difficulties.

If you are working in a hot, dry atmosphere, mix a little more water with your washes to compensate for the speed of drying, or alternatively dampen the surface of your paper before starting to paint. A drop or two of glycerine, available from all art material shops, added to your water jar will also slow down the drying process.

models on the market, and take a length of string with you so that you can attach a convenient brick or rock to weigh it down in breezy weather. If you have difficulty in isolating pleasing compositions from the expanse of landscape, remember to take your viewfinder with you!

MAKING A START

Imagine you have now found a subject that inspires you. However keen you are to start painting, do not be tempted to omit those preliminary exploratory sketches which will help you to decide which is the most pleasing composition. Nothing is more frustrating than discovering a far more interesting viewpoint *after* your painting is complete.

Another problem that needs careful thought is that of shadow movement. Shadows change continuously with the movement of the sun and unless you work very quickly, you must give some thought to this or you may end up with shadows of no consistent direction.

ONLOOKERS

Some painters detest the thought of people looking over their shoulder and find it puts them right off their stroke. This reaction is usually a symptom of excessive modesty, and what they really fear is a critical reaction. They should remember that the average curious onlooker is not only well-disposed towards artists, but usually has little artistic ability of his own and your efforts, whatever you think, will no doubt appear to him as a work of genius. If you are still unconvinced, it is often possible to choose a spot which cannot be approached from the rear, though this stratagem will reduce your chances of locating the ideal viewpoint.

FIGURES IN THE LANDSCAPE

A question that often arises in landscape work is whether or not to include people in your painting. If, for example, you wish to emphasise the feeling of isolation and loneliness of a remote Scottish loch, then obviously you do not need to include people. If, on the other hand, your subject is the sort of scene where you would expect to see people, a street corner for instance, then they should be included.

Unless you have really made a study of the human figure, it would probably be wiser to avoid including any close-ups in which anatomical faults would be all too obvious. Impressions of more distant figures are

THE TWINS SHRIMPING
What struck me about this seaside scene was the depth of tone of the figures viewed against a backdrop of pale sky and shining water. It was a warm evening and the tinge of purple just above the horizon indicated a heat haze. I kept the sky very simple, with just a few summery clouds. The sea was calm and I have shown only one small wave form in any detail. The light catching the tops of the wavelets and the foreground foam are simply the white of the unpainted paper.

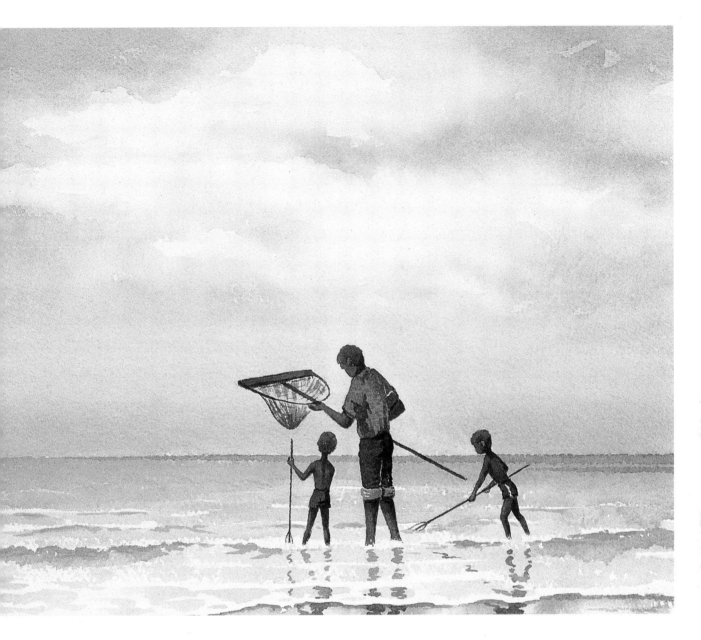

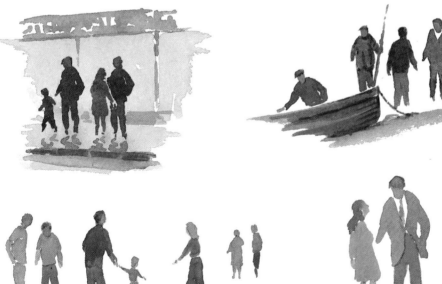

A thorough knowledge of human anatomy is not necessary for the inclusion of a few figures in the landscape, provided you remember that posture is more important than detail. Quick sketchbook studies will help you here – models are not always on hand when required.

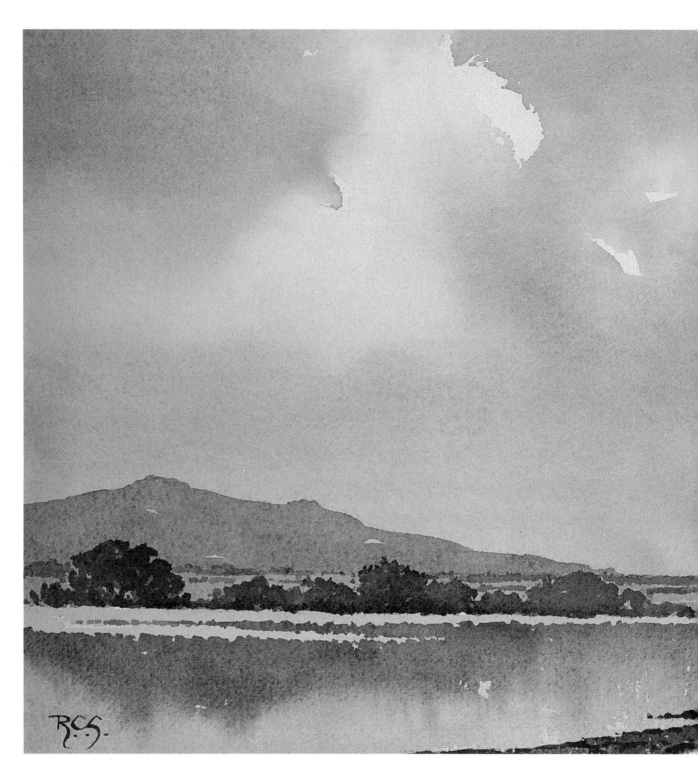

another matter, and it is not too difficult to learn how to suggest groups of people with a few calligraphic dots and dashes.

WATER

Many students find painting water a problem and try to avoid it if they possibly can. This is a pity, because water in a landscape can add an extra dimension to a painting. Of course, it is not always possible to paint water exactly as it appears. In some conditions it can consist of a mass of tiny ripples and any attempt to paint such minute detail would be doomed to failure. In such a case it is better to soften its splintered appearance by viewing it through half-closed eyes and then paint the more diffuse image that results. When ripples are larger and more manageable, they should be painted more literally, but remember that the nearer forms will be of greater depth than the more distant (see page 112). Too many beginners forget that the laws of perspective apply to water as well as dry land. → p.113

THUNDER CLOUD

A quick watercolour sketch in which the object was to capture the fleeting moment. The sky was put in with a single wash and indicates, with some economy, the towering mass of cloud. The sombre blues and greys suggest the sultry lull before the storm while the lower sky indicates a distant rain squall. A line of pale, disturbed water separates the distant shore from its reflection in the calmer water below.

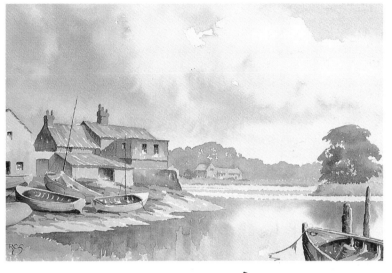

BRANCASTER STAITHE

Those who enjoy painting the coastal scene will find plenty of attractive subject matter along the north Norfolk coast, with its many sea inlets, miles of salt marshes, clustering pan-tiled cottages and rich variety of boats. Today the majority are pleasure boats, but there are still plenty of the sturdy working variety to be seen.

I blended plenty of water into my sky washes to capture the effect of softly billowing cloud. I used single washes whenever possible, the line of distant trees being one example.

The detail on the left of the painting is balanced by the tree on the right and the deep tones of the moored boat below it.

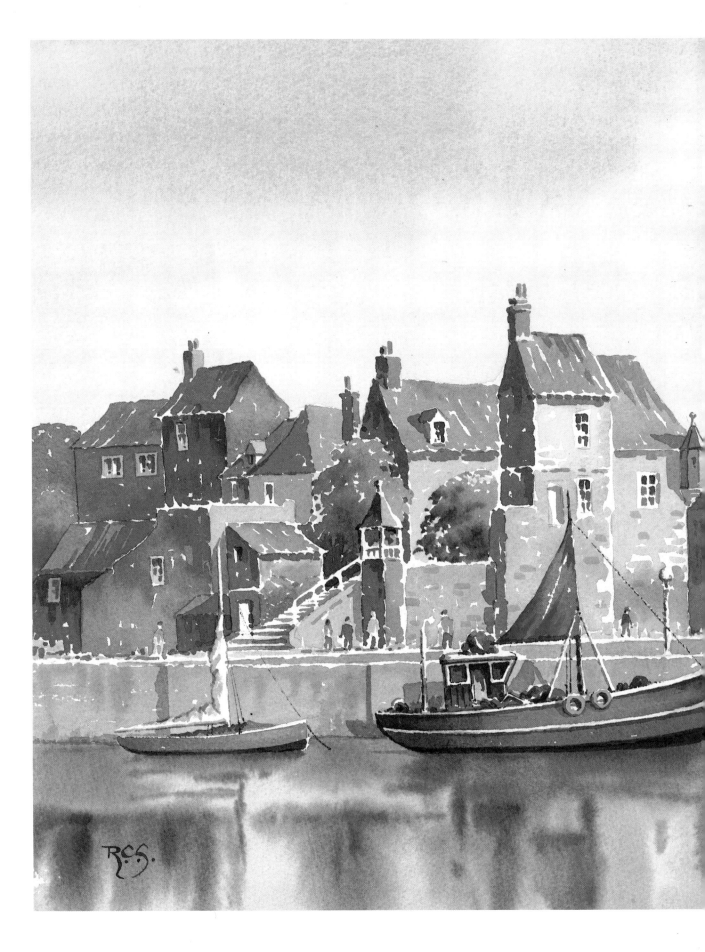

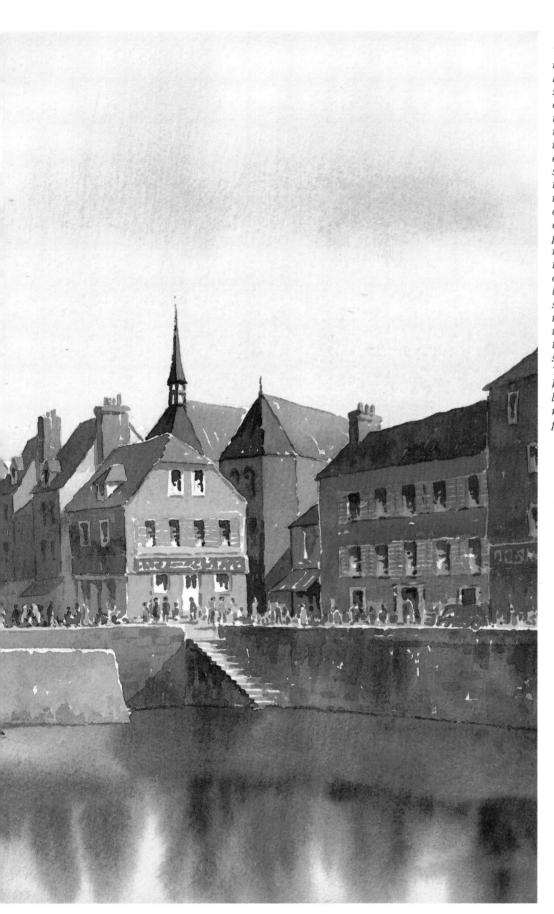

This must be one of the most painted spots in France and it is easy to see why – the jumble of old harbourside houses, the boats and the reflections have an irresistible appeal. The complexity of the subject suggested a very simple treatment of sky and water, to avoid over-complication. The soft, diffuse reflections were painted wet in wet, roughly following the tones and colours of the objects above. The buildings are rather strung out in a line, so it was vital to break them up by emphasising the tonal contrasts of sunlight and shadow. The people, mainly holiday-makers, were little more than multicoloured blobs of paint.

PAINTING IN THE OPEN

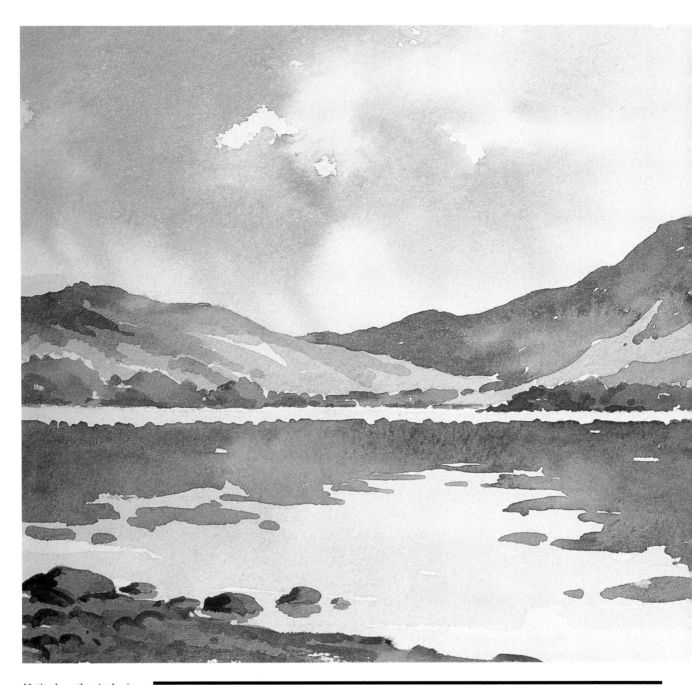

Notice how the ripples in this quick watercolour sketch diminish in size as they recede and how a pale line of wind-ruffled water separates the distant scene from its reflection.

EXERCISES TO TRY

Here are some exercises you can try while working in the open:

1 Choose a sunny day and a subject with plenty of lateral shadow. Make a quick sketch of the scene on watercolour paper, taking particular care to establish the position and form of the shadows.

2 Now apply paint in the form of bold, liquid washes and then add the darker accents, including the shadows. Study the colours in the shadowed areas carefully and do them full justice.

3 Whenever possible make quick impressions in your sketch book of figures that come and go. The more successful ones will serve you well in future paintings.

4 Find a stretch of smooth water in your neighbourhood and practise painting the reflections you see.

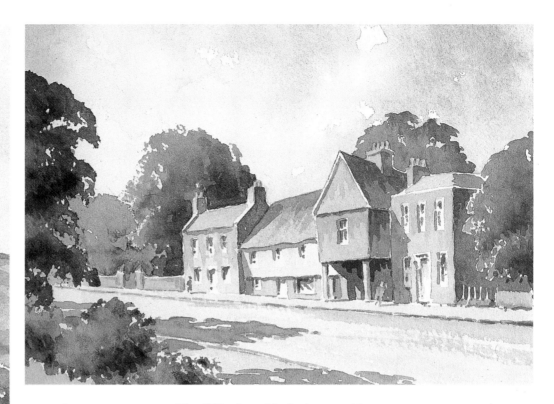

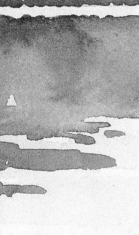

In this watercolour sketch of a village street, a little texturing has been added to the walls and roofs of the buildings to give them a feeling of age and character.

The difficulty with ripples, as with waves, is that they will never keep still to enable you to paint them in comfort. The only solution is to freeze an instant in time in your mind's eye and then paint the remembered image. Remember, too, the old rule which states that lights are reflected darker and darks reflected lighter – in other words there is less tonal contrast in reflections. It holds good most of the time but is not a substitute for careful observation.

Do not worry if your work in the field has a rather unfinished look about it – this is inclined to happen when working conditions are not ideal – but firmly resist the temptation to start tidying things up. However rough the result, if you have managed to capture the feeling and the atmosphere of your subject, then you have succeeded.

MR PERKINS GARDENING

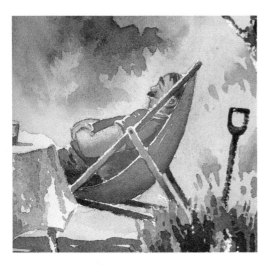

A subject such as this requires quick execution – and, perhaps, a convenient escape route! It is an example of a light-hearted attempt to capture a fleeting moment. The original watercolour sketch was very hastily executed and I have adopted a similar approach here. Working at speed can be a useful exercise in loosening up, particularly if you feel tightness and over-attention to detail beginning to creep into your work.

The figure was seated under the shade of a small tree and so was mainly in shadow. It was necessary, therefore, to ensure that the immediate background remained fairly light, to provide tonal contrast. There was some dappled sunlight on the white tablecloth, so here the background could be a little darker, also for the sake of counterchange.

Palette
raw sienna
light red
ultramarine
Payne's grey
burnt sienna
alizarin crimson

STAGE 1

For once I did not make a number of exploratory sketches – I did not know how much time I had – and so relied upon my first quick impression. The setting was simply sunlit lawn, with some cast shadows in the foreground, and shrubs and trees beyond. I decided to indicate it all in one quick variegated wash, using mainly raw sienna and Payne's grey, with a little alizarin crimson and ultramarine on the left to suggest some wild rhododendrons in flower. I added a few darker accents, wet in wet, and left it all to dry in the sun.

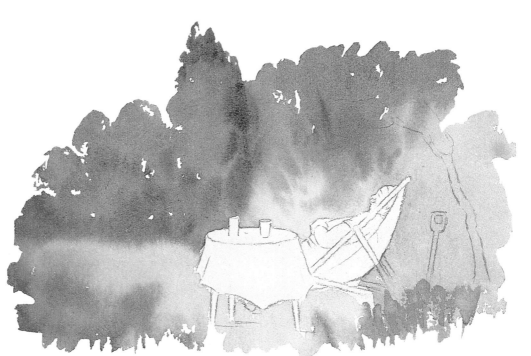

STAGE 2

I decided to add a few darker accents to the background, to give the trees and shrubs a little more form and definition, using a mixture of Payne's grey and burnt sienna on the left and ultramarine and light red on the right. A mixture of Payne's grey and raw sienna served for the shadows on the lawn and, with a little burnt sienna added, for the small foreground tree on the right, while some dry brush work suggested the rough texture of the trunk. For the shadows on the white tablecloth I used ultramarine with a little light red.

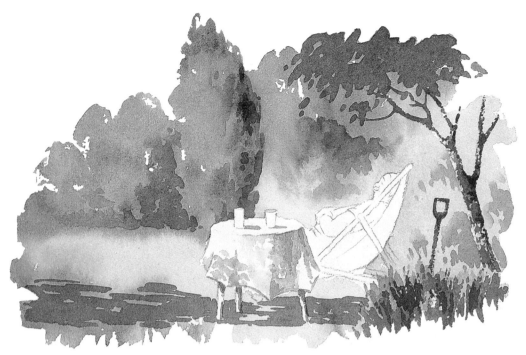

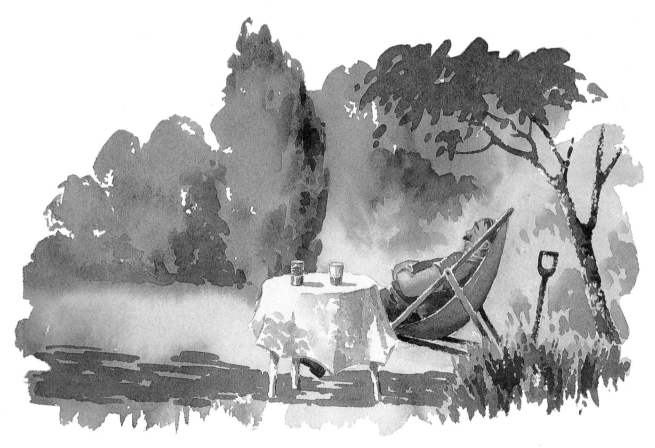

STAGE 3

The recumbent figure was in shadow, so fairly deep tones were required, with a suggestion of reflected light to provide warmth.

I had intentionally left the immediate background very pale and simple so that the deeper colours of the figure would stand out boldly. It also called for

rather more precise treatment than its loosely handled surroundings and this also helped to make it the focal point.

This quick little painting is admittedly

something of a caricature, but is none the worse for that. Painting need not always be a solemn business!

10 To Sum Up

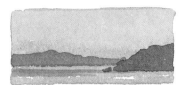

The greater part of this book has been concerned with the technique of watercolour painting, for I believe that every painter anxious to raise his standard and go on to better things must strive to improve the manner in which he applies paint. This is not to imply that technique is the be all and end all of art – that would be very far from the truth. It is, however, an important means to an end, and in the watercolour medium particularly it is hard for an artist to get his message across if he fails, through technical shortcomings, to take full advantage of its wonderful potential. He therefore has to learn how to apply fresh, clear and translucent washes, so that the white of the paper shines through, to impart a luminous quality to his work. This is the first and most important lesson.

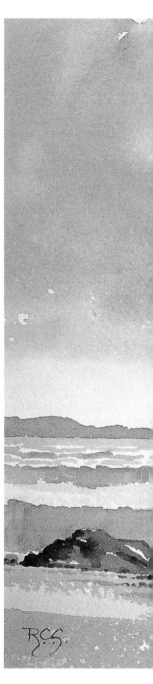

Freshness in watercolour painting is a delicate and vulnerable quality. As we know, it is easily destroyed by attempted alteration, overworking and labouring after detail and it is for this reason that you should not allow yourself to be lured into attempting subjects of excessive complexity. Simple subject matter will allow you to express yourself directly and spontaneously and your work will be all the better for it. As you progress, you will be able to tackle more complex subjects, for you will have acquired the skill to simplify and to describe more complicated forms in a direct and painterly manner. You will find that you rely less and less on careful preliminary drawing and will express yourself with increasingly lively brushwork. Through a growing skill with the brush, your style will crystallise and your work will gain in individuality and originality.

One of the watercolour painter's vital skills, the ability to simplify subject matter and distinguish the essential from the inessential, will have an important bi-product. Instead of the whole of the paper being occupied with detail of one sort or another, there will be plain areas and the painter will learn to value these for the contrast and feeling of space they provide. They will act as a foil to the busy areas and assist in the general pattern of the painting, which, as we noted earlier, stems from the arrangement of its component shapes, colours and tones.

An ability to suggest space is of particular value to the watercolourist primarily interested in landscape and he should never lose an opportunity of studying the work of painters such as Aubrey Phillips who possess this enviable skill. We all learn a great deal by finding out how artists whose work we admire solve problems of composition and technique, and it is fascinating to study their choice of subject matter and the manner in which they tell us something of their personal reaction to it.

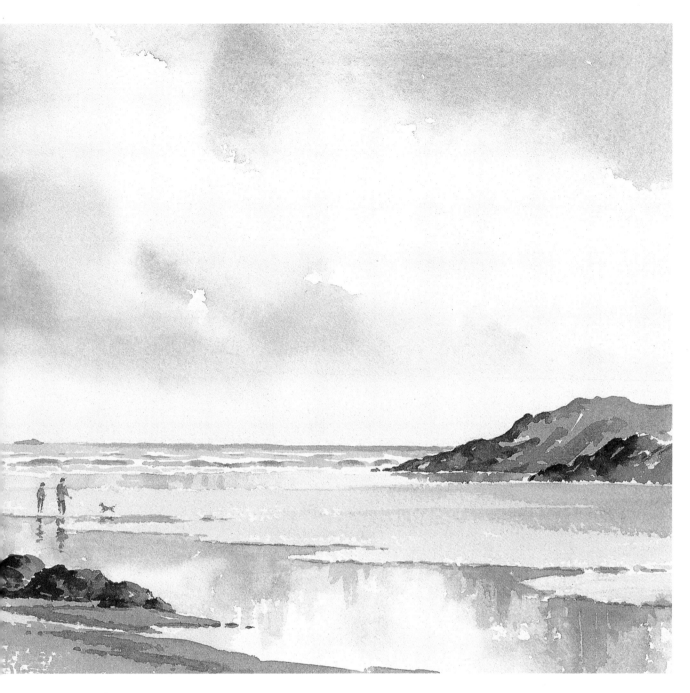

Artists see things in individual and intensely personal ways, and when this is apparent in their painting it can open our eyes and tell us something of their inner feelings.

I find the choice of subject matter of other painters a source of endless fascination, particularly when they see possibilities and find inspiration in the most unpromising scenes. A mean back street, with apparently little to offer, can be touched with magic by the skill and insight of an artist of sensitivity and imagination. Such examples inspire us to look at our surroundings with fresh eyes and to find meaning in the dullest of scenes. The development of our ability to observe greatly enhances our enjoyment and appreciation of

→ p.122

SEA AND SAND,
CORNWALL
In this painting I tried to capture something of the atmosphere of a blustery day by the sea and convey a feeling of freedom and space. The lively sky, the low horizon and the stretch of pale sand right across the paper all make their

contribution and the two small figures also help by providing scale. The technique is loose and fluid and, with the exception of the headland and the foreground rocks, the tones are light. These darker features provide tonal contrast and help to balance the composition.

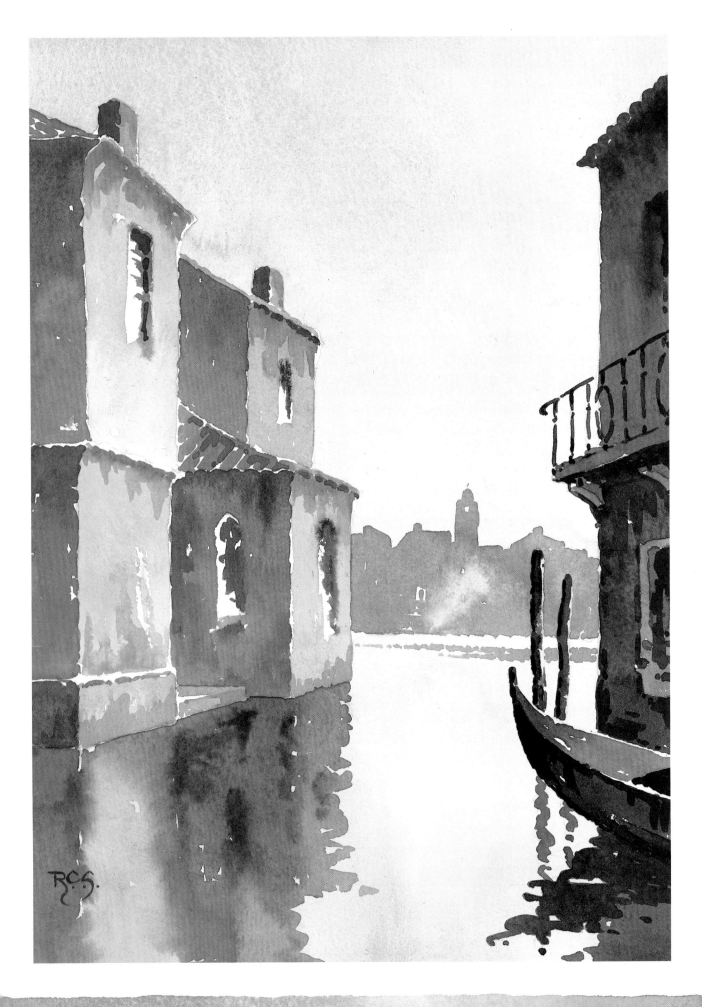

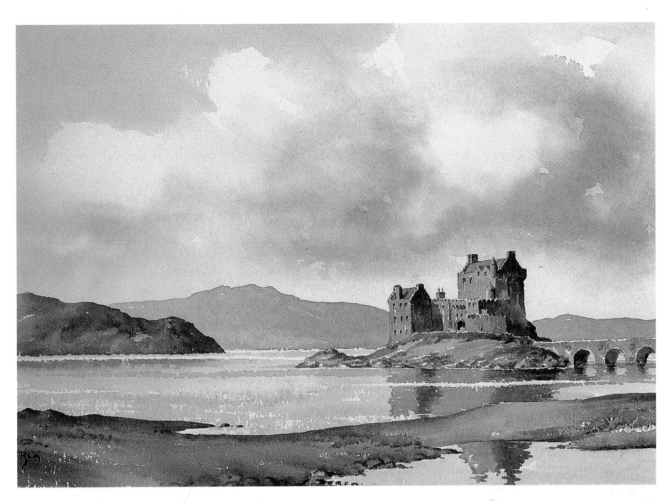

CANAL REFLECTIONS

The distant tower in this simple Venetian scene makes a useful focal point to which all perspective lines seem to lead. The sun was in the right position to provide plenty of tonal contrast in the left-hand building, while the shadowed building on the right, the gondola, the mooring poles and their reflections make a strong statement against the pale sky and smooth water.

THE TEN 'COMMANDMENTS'

1 Preserve freshness at all costs – no watercolour can succeed without it.

2 Avoid over-elaborate subjects – at least until you have acquired the experience to handle them.

3 Learn to simplify and to omit unnecessary detail.

4 Cultivate lively and expressive brushwork.

5 Try to reduce the amount of careful preliminary drawing – this will help you to obey 4.

6 Preserve some plain areas in your work, to provide contrast with the busier ones.

7 Learn to suggest space. Study and analyse the work of the masters.

8 Do not confine yourself to the 'picturesque' – look for possibilities in unlikely subjects.

9 Strive to convey mood, feeling and atmosphere.

10 Only paint when you feel in the mood.

EILEAN DONAN CASTLE

This is another painting in which I made a conscious effort to create the illusion of space. Once again a prominent sky occupies over half the paper and a low viewpoint has the effect of foreshortening the waters of the loch. This foreshortening, combined with the fact that the water stretches right across the paper, helps to emphasise the feeling of space.

The loch was a broken wash of pale grey, and the resulting chains of white dots, where the brush missed the little indentations in the surface of the paper, suggest light sparkling on the water. The much deeper tones of the foreground, the castle and the left-hand promontory provide strong tonal contrast and help to make the water shine.

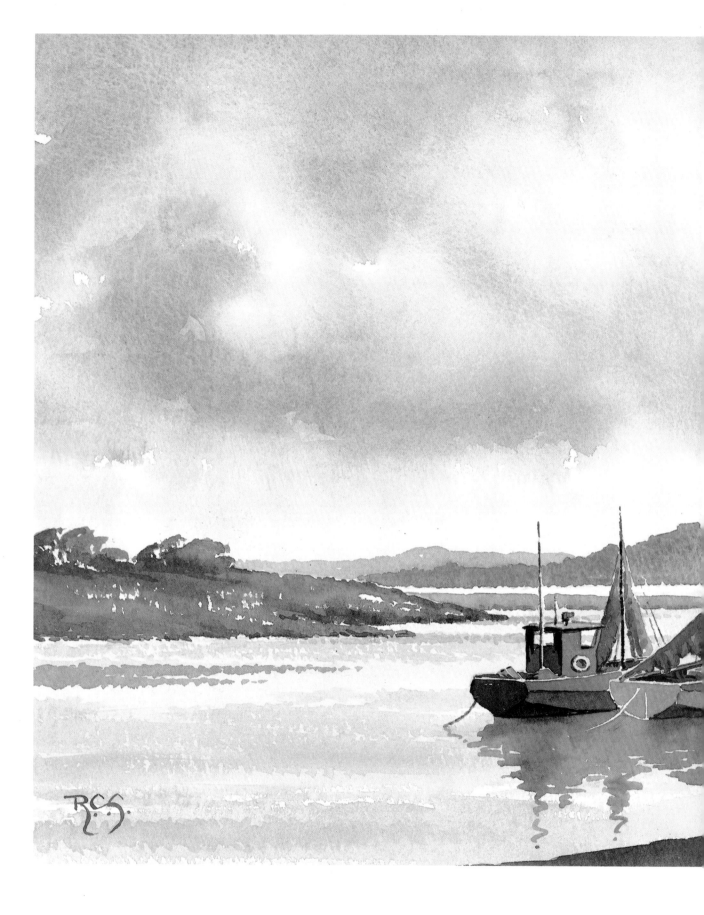

WATERCOLOUR FOR ALL

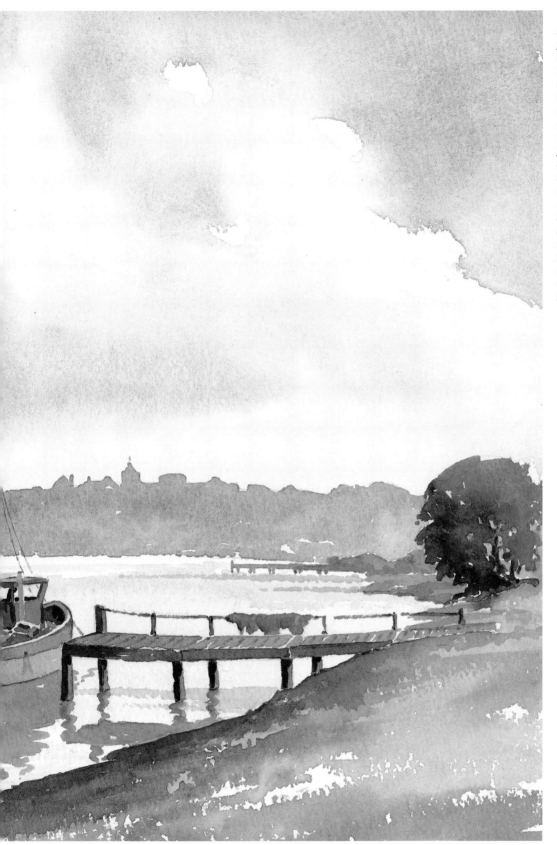

Foreshortened sheets of pale water usually create a feeling of space and the broad estuary of the River Rother at high tide is no exception. The medieval town of Rye, with its splendid church tower making a focal point, is a pale blue-grey silhouette into which several local colours have been introduced. The deep tones of the nearer land forms, the landing stage, the boats and their greenish reflections, contrast with the pale tones of the water and help to make it shine.

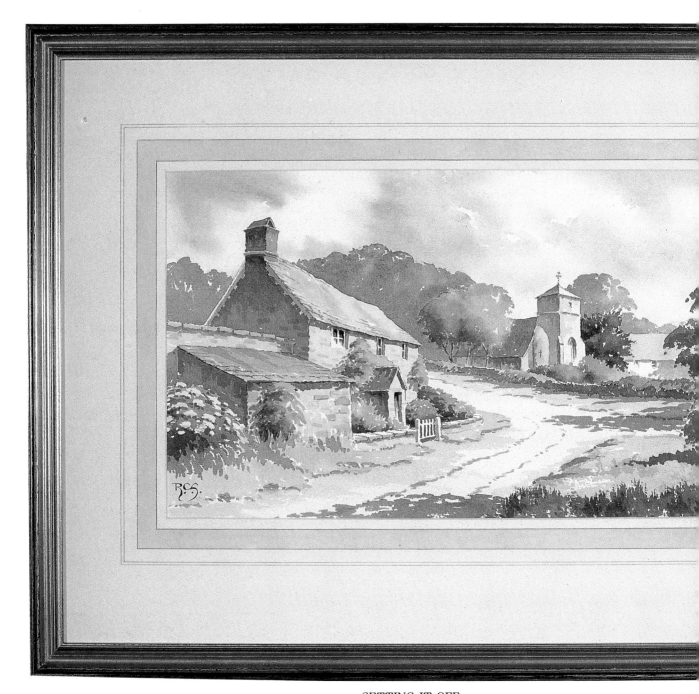

SETTING IT OFF

the world about us, for everything we see begins to acquire meaning and significance. Let us determine, then, to capture mood and feeling in our work, to look at everything with greater insight and, above all, to paint with excitement and enjoyment.

There are many boring but necessary tasks in the workaday world that can be carried out with efficiency but without interest or enjoyment. Painting is not one of them. If the excitement and the enjoyment have gone – stop! Never go on working at a painting just for the sake of finishing it. Far better to wait until inspiration returns, as it surely will, and, in the meantime, seek fresh stimulation from the wonderful world about you.

Once we have produced a painting we feel is worthy of framing, the questions arise – what sort of mount, what type of moulding? Tastes and opinions differ widely, and there can be no single 'correct' answer. After much experimentation I have settled on a traditional format which suits much of my work and, I believe, that of the majority of mainstream watercolourists. This mount and moulding style is illustrated in the painting entitled *Eastleach Martin* (above). The colour of the mount is champagne, which contains less yellow than ivory or cream, and it measures 3½in (9cm) at the top and sides and 4in (10cm) at the bottom. The pale grey-green watercolour wash line is ¾in (2cm) in

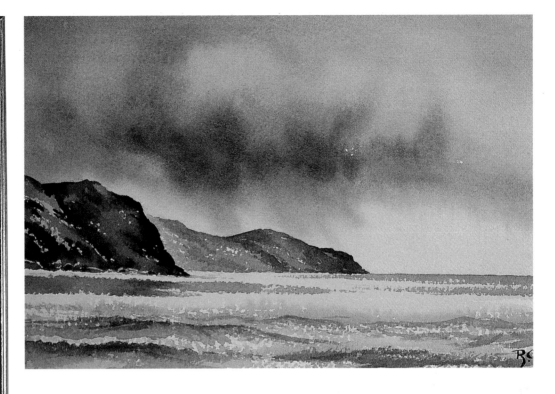

width and a stronger mix of watercolour rather than ink is applied with an adjustable ruling pen to produce the grey lines. The moulding is a 1in (2.5cm) antique gilt.

The width of the mount will naturally vary with the size of the painting and with individual taste. The colour of the wash line can help to pick out some colour in the painting, but should always be kept pale – strong colour never looks attractive and can easily overwhelm the painting. The ruled lines can be just one colour or several different colours – the permutations are endless. For large paintings I use light hardboard backing, for small, grey cardboard.

Frame-making does not appeal to everyone but those naturally handy with a saw may find it a most rewarding occupation.

I do my own mounting and framing partly for economic reasons, partly because I enjoy it and partly because I can do it exactly to my own taste. I do not subscribe to the view that a lot of expensive equipment is necessary. I find a sharp craft knife and a firm metal straight edge, preferably with a rubber inset base, are all I need for cutting mounts, while my modestly priced Swedish mitre cutter produces perfect corners. A simple gadget consisting of four plastic pieces, bound by a nylon cord, clamps the four glued sections of moulding together very satisfactorily and when the wood adhesive has dried, brass-finish panel pins complete the job almost invisibly.

STORM CLOUD, SUTHERLAND
I was impressed by the manner in which the deep slate grey of the cloud formation contrasted with the pale tones of the area of luminous sky just above the horizon, and I tried to capture something of this dramatic counterchange. The soft grey slanting down from the underside of the dark cloud indicates a heavy rainstorm. The land forms are in deep shadow but the blue-grey of the distant headland contrasts with the warmer colouring of the nearer headland, to create a strong feeling of recession and an illusion of space.

EXERCISES TO TRY

A few final suggestions to help you on your way:

1 Select a stretch of country that appeals to you and give yourself 30 minutes to capture its essence in watercolour. This time limit will mean you have to simplify and concentrate on essentials. Pay particular attention to the broad areas of tone and colour.

2 Choose a stretch of coastal scenery, perhaps one with a broad expanse of sand, and try to convey an impression of space.

3 Choose a subject with strong, atmospheric overtones, such as a dockland scene on a murky evening, and concentrate on capturing its mood and feeling.

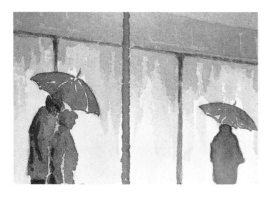

FOG AND DRIZZLE

A group of back-street shops on a miserable evening is not everyone's idea of an inspiring subject, but if one looks at a scene simply as an arrangement of shapes, tones and colours and nothing more, then what it actually *is* ceases to matter. On another plane, the effects of light shining through mist and reflected in a wet surface have a different but equally strong appeal. There is also the challenge of making something interesting of unlikely subject matter. If we keep these considerations in view and cultivate an open and receptive mind, our imagination will begin to enliven the most unpromising material and we will realise that idyllic landscapes are not the only suitable subjects for watercolour.

This particular scene was painted from memory. My objective was to capture something of the halo effect of street lights in the mist and lights reflected on a wet road.

Palette
raw sienna
light red
ultramarine
burnt sienna

STAGE 1

I adopted a fairly low viewpoint and sketched in the main lines of the buildings and road. The figures were mostly placed against rectangles of light representing shop windows. In contrast to the coldness of the evening, the foggy air imparted a warmth to the overall colour, and this was reinforced by the artificial light from the shop fronts. I prepared two washes for the sky and the misty area to the right of the buildings. The first was dilute raw sienna and light red, for the area immediately round the street light, and the second was a rather stronger mix of ultramarine and light red. I applied these variegated washes quickly and boldly and achieved a gradual transition from the warm, pale tone, by the source of light, to the cooler, deeper colour beyond.

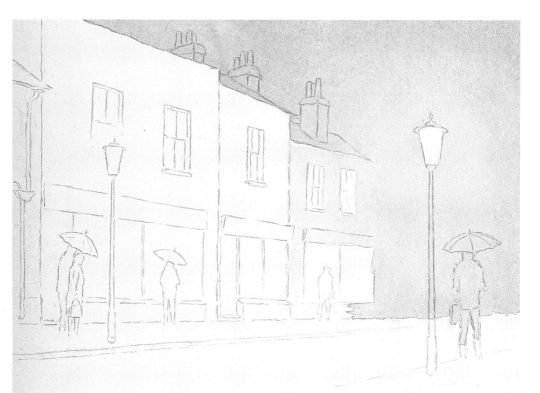

STAGE 2

I began by painting the first floor windows in pale raw sienna with a touch of light red to suggest curtains. I used the same colours for the shop fronts but added rather more warmth. The fronts of the buildings were varying mixes of burnt sienna, light red and ultramarine, with a paler area of raw sienna and light red to represent the misty radiance round the left-hand street light. I then added darker accents with various combinations of the same range of colours to indicate weather-staining on the fronts of the buildings and such details as glazing bars, rain pipes, various small areas of shadow and a little detailed brickwork.

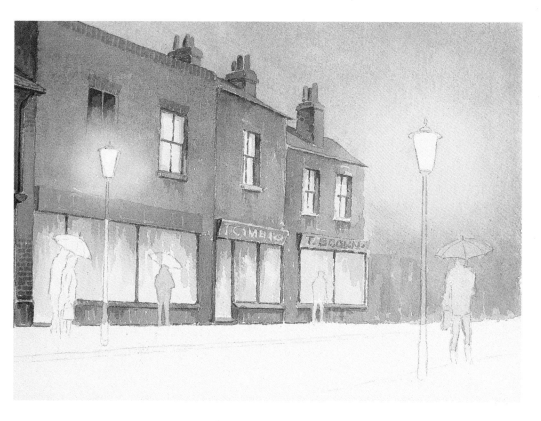

STAGE 3

I now began to paint in the five figures and their umbrellas. The more distant ones are just deep grey silhouettes and the others show only slightly more detail. I decided to make the reflections in the wet road soft edged rather than attempt any sort of mirror image, firstly because the unevenness of the surface would break up anything too precise, and secondly, because I did not want the road to compete with the rest of the painting.

I prepared several washes, corresponding to the colours of the objects above, and applied them with quick, vertical brushstrokes so that they merged together. As the paper was beginning to dry, I added a few darker accents in a deep grey (ultramarine and light red) and let the whole thing dry. I then added the kerbstones, some indication of the paving slabs and a few wheel tracks in the wet surface of the road.

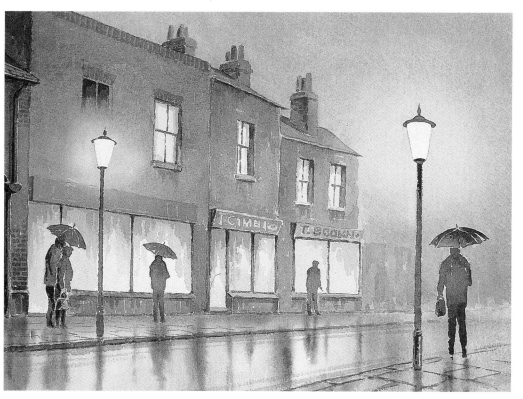

GLOSSARY

Aerial perspective
Water vapour, smoke and dust in the atmosphere make distant objects appear pale and greyish. This makes them recede and is termed aerial perspective.

After image
If you look fixedly at a patch of colour and then transfer your gaze to a white surface, you will see that colour's complementary, or opposite (sometimes called the after image).

Broken colours
Colours containing all three primaries. When the proportions are roughly equal, dull browns and greys result. Varying the proportions can produce subtle and often beautiful colours.

Cold press
The unheated flat metal plate applied to sheets of paper in the manufacturing process to produce a NOT surface.

Colour temperatures
Reds and oranges are said to be hot colours (ie of high temperature), blues and greys, cool (ie of low temperature).

Complementary colour
This simply means opposite colour, or colour occupying the opposite position on the colour wheel (eg red and green, purple and yellow).

Composition
The arrangement of the elements of a subject on the support. If the composition is good, the arrangement will appear harmonious.

Counterchange
The placing of lights against darks and darks against lights to achieve tonal contrast.

Definition
Some objects in the landscape may appear hard edged, some soft edged. The term definition refers to their degree of clarity.

Flowering
If a liquid pigment is applied to a drying wash, the pigment will be carried by capillary action into that wash and deposited in unsightly concentrations.

Foreshortening
If a plane is viewed obliquely, its depth appears much reduced. Thus a distant field may appear as a thin strip, the effect of foreshortening.

Golden mean/ golden section
The position on a rectangular support, found by geometric construction held to possess special compositional significance for the placement of important features.

Hot press
The heated flat metal plate applied to sheets of paper in the manufacturing process to produce a smooth surface.

Linear perspective
A system of geometric constructions for achieving accurate recession, based on the fact that objects appear progressively smaller with distance.

Local colour
The true colour of an object when unaffected by the quality of the light or shade or the proximity of other objects.

Luminosity
The quality of emitting light. In watercolour, clear washes permit the white of the paper to shine through, creating an impression of light.

Masking fluid
A form of liquid latex applied to watercolour paper to protect specified areas from overall washes. When everything is dry, the latex can be removed with the forefinger.

Passage
The term given to a particular section of a painting, particularly a homogeneous area such as a single wash.

Patina
Surface appearance or texture. In the watercolour context, a good quality paper will reveal a pleasing patina when clear washes are applied.

Primary colour
The three primary colours are red, yellow and blue, from which all the other colours are derived.

Recession
If an artist has conveyed a feeling of recession, he has succeeded in making the distance appear distant and the foreground advanced.

Secondary colour
The colour that results from mixing two primaries (eg red and yellow make orange, blue and yellow make green).

Size
In the watercolour context, a weak glue used in the manufacture of paper. Generally speaking, the greater the amount used, the harder and less absorbent the surface.

Support
The name given to any paper, board, canvas etc, used for drawing and painting.

Tertiary colour
Colour formed by mixing all three primaries. Sometimes called broken colour.

Tightness
A term given to the quality of a very precise and laboured painting.

Tonal contrast
The effect obtained by placing lights and darks in close proximity.

Tonal weight
Depth of colour. If one says the tonal weight of a painting is all on one side, it means the darker colours are concentrated there.

Tone
In art, tone simply means lightness or darkness, not colour as in popular usage.

Vanishing point
The point on the true horizon at which pairs of parallel lines on a level plane will appear to converge when projected.

Wet in wet
The technique of painting into a wash that is still wet to achieve a soft-edged effect.

INDEX

Numbers in **bold** denote illustrations

Accuracy, 68, 83
After image, 26
Alizarin crimson, 15
Alterations, 18, 19, 83, 116
Animals, **13**, 43, **43**
Atmosphere, 64, 66, 119 *see also* Mood
Autumn Meadow, **96**

Backing, 123
Bamburgh Castle, **67**
Barges, 76, **76**
Barns, 34–5, **34–5**
Beached Boat, **18**
Bend in the River, **69**
Berkshire Downs, **8–9**
Bluestone Farm, Norfolk, 22–3, **22–3**
Boats, 18, **28–9**, 44, 46, **46–9**, 49, 68, **68**, **74–5**, **83**, **88**, **94–5**, **104–5**, **108–11**, **120–1**
Brancaster Staithe, **108–9**
Bridges, **30–1**, 68, **68**, **78–9**
Brushes, 16–17, **17**, 88
  Care of, 73
  Chinese, 17, **17**
  Size, 17
Brushwork, 7, 16, 20, 21, 68, 71, 77, 116, 119
  Dry, 19, 60, 63, 89, 115
Buildings, 20, 22–3, **22–3**, **38–40**, 40, 41, 45, **46–55**, **59**, 62–3, **62–3**, 67, **67**, 68, **71**, **80–1**, 81, 82, **90–1**, **110–11**, **124–5**
Burnt umber, 15
Bushes, 12, **12**, 13, **13**, **61**, 89, **89**, 91

Cadgwith Cove, **104–5**
Cadmium orange/ yellow, 15
Calm Anchorage, 46–9, **46–9**
Castles, 67, **67**, **118–19**
Cathedral of the Marshes, The, **76–7**
Cauliflowering *see* Flowering

Chimneys, **60**, **62–3**
Chinese white, 84
Christmas Eve, 12–13, **12–13**
Churches, **30–1**, 34–5, **34–5**, **38–9**, **59**, 62–3, **62–3**, 76–7, **76–7**, 80–1, **80–1**, **120–1**
Clarity, 6, 7
Cliffs, 33, **33**, **66**, 67
Clouds, **8–10**, **20**, 22, **22–3**, **74–6**, 76, **78–9**, 83–4, **83–4**, 89, 90, **108–9**, **123**
Coastal scenes, **40**, 44, **46–9**, **66**, **74–6**, **83**, **94–5**, **104–11**, **116–17**, 123 *see also individual headings*
Cockling, 19, 20
Colours, 15, 16, 24–35 *see also* Palette
  Complementary, 26–7, 29, 33, 66
  Primary, 15, 25
  Secondary, 15, 25
  Temperature, 26
  Tertiary/broken, 15, 25
  Wheel, **25**, 26
Composition, 7, 50–63, 66, 68, 106
  Faults, 56–9
Contrast, 20, 22, 26–7, **28–9**, 29, 31, 33, **38–9**, **50–1**, 66, 67, 70, 101, **104–5**, **110–11**, 114–15, **116–19**, 119, 123
Cornish Harbour, **40**
Cotswolds, **60–3**, 67
Cotswold Village Street, **67**
Cottages, 34–5, **34–5**, **60–3**, **104–5**
Cottages at Filkins, 60–3, **60–3**

Damping, 22, 97, 106
Dartmoor Farm, **10**
Demonstrations, 12–13, 22–3, 34–5, 46–9, 60–3, 70–1, 80–1, 90–1, 100–1, 114–15, 124–5

Depth, 26, 44 *see also* Recession
Derwentwater, **40–1**
Design, 50–63, 66
Detail, 7, 64, 67, 81, 83, 96, 119
Distances, 44 *see also* Recession
Dockland, 123
Draughtsmanship, 68
Drawing board, 106
  Angle, 77
Drying, 7, 33, 73, 84, 93, 96, 106
Dunsfold Church, 34–5, **34–5**

Easel, 106
Eastleach Martin, **122–3**
Ebb Tide, Norfolk, **44**
Edge definition, 12, 93, **94–6**, 96
Eilean Donan Castle, **118–19**
Equipment, 14–21
  Framing, 123
  Outdoor, 103, 106
Essex Boatyard, **74–5**
Estuary, **46–9**
Euclid, 54
Evening in Knole Park, **42–3**
Evening Light, Rye, **88**
Evening Mists, **92**
Exercises, 21, 31, 45, 59, 69, 79, 89, 97, 112, 123

Farm Buildings at Heaverham, **90–1**
Farm near Shipbourne, **11**
Farm Track, **18**
Farmhouses, **10**, 12–13, **12–13**, 22–3, **22–3**
Farms, **7**, **10–13**, 20, 22–3, **22–3**, **50–3**, **70–1**, **90–1**, **90–1**
Fences, 23, **23**, 37
Fields, 10, 21, 23, 68, 70, **70–1**, 82, **96**, **101** *see also* Grass; Plough-land
Figures, 12, 13, **13**, 26, **26–7**, 31, 35, **35**, 44, 66, 67, 92, **92**,

104–7, 106, 108, **110–11**, 112, 114–15, **114–17**, **124–5**
Fishermen's huts, 46–7, **46–7**
Flood Tide Below Rye, **120–1**
Flowering, 84, 90, 93, 97
Flowers, 15, 18, **18**
Fog and Drizzle, **124–5**
Foliage, 18, **18**, 20, 23, 30, 31, 85 *see also* Bushes; Trees
Foreground, 10–12, 23, 30, 31, 45, 60, 61, 66, 67, **81**, **85**, 88, **88**, **91**, **101**
Frames/Framing, 123
Freshness, 6, 7, 64, 72, 73, 83, 116, 119

Garden, **114–15**
Gates, 12, **12**, 35, **35**, 101
Geometry, 36, 54
Glycerine, 106
Golden mean/section, 54
Gondolas, 80, **80–1**
Grand Canal, The, **80–1**
Grass, 10, **28–9**, 31, 33, 47, **47**, **61**, 85, **85**, **91**
Gravestones, 60, **62–3**
Gulls, 84

Halfpenny Bridge, The, **78–9**
Hedges, **8–9**, 12, 13, **13**, 23, **23**, 31, **34–5**, 68, **71**, **101**
Hills, 34–5, **34–5**, **71**, 79, **89**, 97
Honfleur, **110–11**
Horizon, 22, 37, 40, 41, 45, **46**, 56, 68, 70, **76–7**
Houses, 12, **30–1**, 41, **54**, **60–3**, **76–7**, 77, **110–11** *see also* Farmhouses
Humidity, 84, 96

Impressionists, 27

Kentish Farmyard, 70–1, **70–1**

La Grande Rue, La Roque, **55**
Lake District, **40–1**
Landing stage, **88**, **120–1**
Landscapes, 6, 64, 68 *see also individual headings*
Lanes, 12, **12**, 82
La Roque sur Ceze, **55**
Lifting out, colour, 84, 97
Light, 30, 33, 82, 92
  Evening, **42–3**, **67**, 82, **88**, 90–1, **92**
Light red, 12, 15, 22, 34, 46, 60, 70, 80, 90, 124
Lochs, **118–19**
Locomotive, railway, 103

Mail van, **59**
Marshes, **108–9**
Masking fluid, 43, 60, 72, 84, 85, 88
  Tape, 72, 76
Masts, 46, **46**
Mediterranean, 15
Medway Bridge, **30–1**
Mining Valley, **89**
Mirror, use of, 41
Mist, 12, 26, **40–3**, 45, **68**, 69, 85, 92–101, **92**, **94–5**, **98–101** *see also individual headings*
Misty Woodland, **45**
Montmartre, **38–9**
Mood, 119, 122, 123 *see also* Atmosphere
Moorland, **10**
Moulding, 122–3
Mountains, 40, **40–1**
Mounting, 122–3
Mr Perkins Gardening, 114–15, **114–15**
Muddiness, 6, 30, 72, 83

Near Fordcombe, **52–3**
Net Sheds of Old Hastings, **83**
Norfolk, **22–3**, 44, **108–9**
North Downs, 34–5, **34–5**, **71**

Onlookers, 106
Outdoors, painting, 102–15

Paints, 14, 15
Palettes, 12, 15, 22, 34, 46, 60, 70, 80, 90, 124
Paper, 19, 88, 96
  Arches, 13
  NOT/CP, 18, 19
  Rough, 19, 88
  Smooth/HP, 19
  Stretching, 19, 20
  Tinted, 30
Patchiness, 79
Payne's grey, 9, 12, 15, 22, 34, 60, 70, 90
Pen and ink work, 19
Pencil, aquarelle, 18
Perspective, 36–49, 70, 108
  Aerial, **41–3**, 44, **45**, 93
  Linear, 36–41, **38–40**, 44, 93
Phillips, Aubrey, 116
Photographs, 102
Planning, 7, 10–11 *see also* Composition
Plough-land, **8–9**, 23, **71**
Pointillism, 27
Pond, farm, **50–1**, **90–1**
Pool of London, The, **68**
Prussian blue, 15

Rain, **40–1**, **123–5**
Recession, 26, **27**, 34, 44, **71**, **80–1**, 93, **94–5**, 123
Reflections, 31, **31–3**, 44, 46, 47, **47–51**, 49, **66**, 67, 69, **69**, **74–6**, **80–1**, **90–1**, **94–5**, **109–13**, **124–5**
Rhododendron, **18**
Rigger, 17, **17**
Ripples, **49**, 80, **80**, 108, **112–13**
River, 44, **68–9**, 69, **78–9**, **120–1**
Roads, **38–9**, **52–3**, **55**, **59**, **124–5**
Rocks, 33, **33**, 89, **89**, **116–17**
Roofs, **23**, 55, 70, **71**, **90–1**, 91, 103, **113**
Rye, **88**, **120–1**

Sand, 44, **44**, **66–7**, **116–17**, 123
Sea, 33, **33**, **66–7**, 76, **76**, **83**, **94–5**, **116–17**
Sea Mists, **94–5**
Sea and Sand, Cornwall, **116–17**
Seurat, 27
Seven Sisters, The, **66**

Shadows, 13, **13**, 21–3, **27**, 30, **34–5**, **55**, 57, **63**, 66, 68, **71**, 76, 91, **96**, 106, 112, **114–15**
Shingle, **66**, 67, 83, **83**
Shops, **124–5**
Sienna, burnt/raw, 12, 15, 22, 34, 46, 60, 70, 80, 90, 124
Sketches, 51, 54, **55**, 59, 60, 67, 68, **69**, 102, 106, 112
Sky, **8–9**, 12, **12**, **16**, 17, **18**, 21, 22, **22–3**, **27**, 30, **33–5**, 46, **46**, **60**, 66, **67**, **72–3**, 76–9, 82–4, **83**, **90–1**, 97, 101, **116–19**
Slack Tide, **76**
Smoke, **68**
Snow, 12, 13, 27, **27**
Snow over the Downs, 21, **27**
Space, 116, **116–19**, 119, 123
Speed, 6, 18, 67, 96
Storm Cloud, Sutherland, **123**
Streets, **55**, **59**, 117, **124–5**
  Village, **59**, **67**, **113**
Stretching, 19, 20
Stripiness, 78
Stubble, 89
Subjects, 51, 64–71, 116, 119
  Choosing, 65–7, 116–17, 122
  Developing, 68
  Urban, 69, 117
Summerford Farm, Withyham, **7**
Sun, 20, 67, **67**, **72–3**, **72–3**, 106 *see also* Light

Techniques, 19, 82–102
Temperature, 84
  Colour, 26
Texture, paper, 19
Texturing, 11, 23, 29, 31, 33, 89, 91, 113
Thunder Cloud, **109**
Tips, 7, 10, 26, 41, 66, 68
Tone, 6, 29, 33, 44, 57, 64, 68
Track, farm, **18**, 23, **50–1**, **90–1**, **101**
Translucence, 72–3, 116
Trees, 12, **12**, 13, **13**, 21, 23, **30–5**, **42–3**, **45**, **61**, 66, 68, **69**, **71**, 79, 82, 85, **85**, **89**, **91–2**, 92–3, 97, **97**, **100–1**
Trees in the Mist, **100–1**
Turner, J.M.W., 92
Twins Shrimping, The, **106–7**

Ultramarine, 12, 15, 22, 34, 46, 60, 70, 80, 90, 124

Vanishing point, 37, 40, 41, 45 *see also* Horizon
Venice, **80–1**
Viewfinder, 51, 65, 69, 106
Villages, **60–1**
  Green, **34–5**
  Street, **59**, **67**, **113**

Walls, **61–3**, 103
Wash line, 122–3
Washes, 6, 19, 21–3, 30, 72–91, 116
  Broken, 11, **11**, 19, 21, 23, 67, 83, 88, **88–9**, 89, 91
  Flat, 76–7, 79, **89**
  Graded, 78, 79
  Mixing/preparation, 6, 7, 12
  Variegated, 78–80, 82–3, 85, 89
Water **29**, **31–3**, 33, 46–7, **46–9**, 49, **68**, **69**, **78–81**, 79, 82, **88**, **90–1**, **96**, 97, 108, **108–13**, 112–13, **118–21**
Water, for painting, 72–3
Wealden Farm, **50–1**
Welsh Townscape, **54**
Westminster Bridge, **16**
Wet in wet, 12, **12**, 23, 45, 61, 76, 78, 80, 83–4, 89, 90, 92, 93–101, **93–7**, **100–1**, **110–11**, **114–15**
  Timing, 83–4, 96–7, 100
Willow, **96**
Wiltshire Farm, **20**
Winsor blue, 34, 46, 60, 80, 90
Winter on the Yorkshire Moors, **11**
Winter Sun, **72–3**
Wintry scenes, 12–13, **12–13**, **27**, **72–3**
Woodland, **8–9**, **32–3**, 45, 66, **71**, **85**, 92, 92, 93, **97**
Woodland Pool, **85**
Woodland Stream, **32–3**
Woodland Track, 93, 96, **97**
Work and Play, **28–9**

Yacht, **48–9**, 49